The Creative Writer's Handbook

the text of this book is printed
on 100% recycled paper

The Creative Writer's Handbook

What to Write, How to Write It, Where to Sell It

Second Edition

Isabelle Ziegler

BARNES & NOBLE BOOKS

A DIVISION OF HARPER & ROW, PUBLISHERS

New York, Hagerstown, San Francisco, London

To Margaret

First BARNES & NOBLE BOOKS edition published 1975.

LIBRARY OF CONGRESS CATALOG CARD NUMBER: 74-9257

STANDARD BOOK NUMBER: 06-463421-3

76 77 78 10 9 8 7 6 5 4 3 2

Contents

1

The Creative Writer

People write for two primary reasons: to be read and to make money. What an author writes is based on his purpose: to entertain, to instruct, or to affect his readers. How he writes depends upon his character, personality, zest, and capacity. How a person writes reflects what he himself is.

The author who claims to write only for himself and to please himself accomplishes only that in the end. He is the amateur who never becomes a professional. His need to write may be therapeutic. Once he has put his torment and frustrations on paper, he can walk happily away from writing and take up a more fitting trade or profession. Some authors who claim to write only for themselves do not speak honestly but are protecting themselves against possible failure. Such a writer—when he has finished his story or play—begins to think about being published and read.

What and how a person writes determine whether or not he is going to be published and if he is, by whom. Every beginning writer dreams of finding an editor or publisher who will recognize his genius, show him the way, and push or pull him toward his goal, publication. In the past this happened, though more rarely than writers believe. Today's editors and publishers cannot afford to wait for the writer's maturity. They would like to develop genius and subsidize its growth, but publication costs, the small margin of profit, competition with other media, and the unpredictability of public taste demand writers who are ready to be published today, writers who know what to write and how to write it.

This demand is responsible for the increasing number of creative-writing classes in colleges and universities, writing clubs, conferences, and regional creative-writing institutes. The purpose of this book, the result of the writer's long experience in conducting college classes in creative writing, is to help meet the demand.

I use the word "conducting" because creative writing cannot be taught; it can only be learned. A teacher cannot tell an individual how to write; he can tell him only how to write better. The teacher can conduct or guide or direct; he can save the writer time—perhaps years—by showing him the shortcuts and by helping him solve the technical problems that use up time and energy. He can help him overcome emotional blocks that keep him from writing. The teacher can even strike a match and set the writer afire. However, the flame itself is not in the teacher but in the writer.

All writing that is not directly copied from another source is creative. A letter is creative. An advertising slogan is creative. Whatever goes through the mind of a human being and is altered by it is creative. The difference among writers lies in their quality, their purpose, their effect. The difference between *Hamlet* and an episode of *Gunsmoke* is the difference in the quality of the writing style, the purpose of the dramatic form, and the effect of the play on the audience. The writer may assume rightfully that he is creative, but he must determine where he belongs in the creative field; he must discover his potential as well as his limitations.

QUESTIONS FOR BEGINNING WRITERS

The writer who has had little or no experience in creative writing should ask himself certain questions.
1. Where do I fit in, where do I belong in the vast field of writing? What is my heritage, my experience? Am I a traditionalist or an idol smasher? Am I going to use the past, or am I among the innovators?
2. What is my particular talent? Is it for fiction or nonfiction? Do I have a strong sense of theater? Can I become a poet?
3. What do I know about the market? What publications do I

want to or can I write for? If I have a facile style and not too profound an insight, am I going to try to write for literary reviews? If I sneer at the stories of the *Ladies' Home Journal*, am I going to try to write for it anyhow? Am I going to try to write for magazines I have never read?

CHARACTERISTICS OF WRITERS

The writer has many things to think about, wonder about, ponder on.

1. He doesn't have to like people, but he must be profoundly, passionately interested in them.

2. The writer must have an equally passionate desire to make other people see what he sees, hear what he hears.

3. He must be sensitive to the human condition and moved to express his feelings about it.

4. He must have a passion for words so that phrases, sentences, and rhythms haunt him.

5. As a person he must be profoundly committed to what he is writing; as an artist he must be detached from it as he learns to recognize what is good and what is bad about his writing.

6. The writer needs to be born this morning and again tomorrow morning. He needs to look at familiar faces as if he had never seen them. He should drive his car to wherever he is going as if it were the first time. He should look at the face of the supermarket checker as if she, too, had been born this morning.

7. He must learn that writing is rewriting. He must be able to cut away at his manuscript without quivering, to carve up his child without flinching.

8. He must acquire a deep concern for details. This concern often makes the difference between a successful and an unsuccessful story or article.

9. A person must realize that writing is a daily routine, not the result of an occasional inspiration. He has to find the time every day to sit down and write. Keeping a journal is one way of sitting down and writing. The beginning writer cannot use his job as an excuse for not writing.

10. He must realize that only a small number of writers are able to make a living by writing. They are few compared to those who have other professions, trades, or jobs.

11. He must admit, finally, that there are no excuses, that the only reason he isn't writing is because he doesn't want to. People write successfully everywhere, under all conditions and with all kinds of handicaps.

12. Occasionally he will stop in anguish and tell himself that everything has been said, all the tales have been told. He must remind himself that the story of Romeo and Juliet had been told by an Italian writer of novellas, but that Shakespeare told it better, and that the same plot was retold later in the form of *Abie's Irish Rose* and again in *West Side Story*.

13. The writer must learn to live with his rejection slips, use them for scrap paper, not label them "End of the World." He can avoid many rejection slips by knowing the market. He should not, of course, be sending manuscripts to a magazine that went out of existence seven years ago.

14. The writer must learn how to handle the problem of loneliness, for writing is a lonely profession. It is one road a person must walk alone.

PROBLEMS OF WRITERS

This book is concerned with problems that writers have in common. Obviously, no two writers are alike. In a group of twenty people there will be twenty levels of writing. Nevertheless, at some time all twenty have the same problems to solve: What point of view should I use? What is wrong with the dialogue? Why does the character fail to come off? Am I trying to write a novel from material that has the scope of a short story? How valid is this particular flashback?

THE PURPOSE OF THIS BOOK

This book is designed to help you cope with the problems that arise in the everyday work of writing. It contains a great deal of practical information about techniques, literary terms, publications, and markets. It is not a book of theory about writing, but rather a how-to book, a guidebook that tells how, where, when, and why.

2

The Writer's Field: Fiction and Nonfiction

The art of writing presents to the beginner a bewildering choice of fields: fiction or nonfiction, novels or films or plays, essays or biographies. Since few writers are successful in more than one field, the beginner will save a great deal of time and effort by discovering early where his talents lie and by deciding in which particular field he wishes to concentrate his efforts. No matter which field he chooses to labor in, the writer will be limited only by his talent and his industry.

THE FICTION WRITER

Fiction is an old word in the English language. It is derived from a verb meaning "to make," "to form," and sometimes "to feign." Unlike the nonfiction writer who puts together facts, data, reports, and truths as he sees them, the novelist, playwright, or short-story writer makes, forms, and feigns. Through what he has made up, he arrives at a truth or enables his reader to arrive at one.

The Novelist

The novelist has many ways to go, depending on his kind of talent. He may write the short, intense vertical novel with psychological and symbolic overtones; the extended panoramic novel which involves generations of people or a vast situation like a war; the historical novel; the biographical or autobiographical novel; science fiction; the mystery, adventure, or Western novel, published in quantities in paperbacks.

The literary novel today is a slim story, intense, brief, economical, and generally told from one person's point of view. The writer swiftly sets his character down into a dramatic situation and just as swiftly moves him to the conclusion. Structurally, this is called the vertical novel, as opposed to the more leisurely, spreading out horizontal novel. Albert Camus' *The Stranger* and Bernard Malamud's *The Fixer* are vertical novels. The protagonist of each is placed in a dramatic situation which moves directly and relentlessly to an inevitable conclusion. The stranger commits a murder for which it seems no other man would have been executed. He is condemned in part for absurd reasons quite outside the crime. (For example, he did not weep at his mother's funeral.) Nevertheless, his condemnation is inevitable. Another vertical novel is William Golding's *Lord of the Flies*. The dramatic situation here is that of a group of boys who find themselves isolated on an island. Golding quickly tells his story as the boys who represent civilization succumb to the violent impulses within themselves.

The new novel is in revolt against all preceding novel forms (romantic, realistic, picaresque, social-protest). The protagonists are nonheroes or anti-heroes who are revealed generally as smaller than life or just as small as life. As existentialists, they have no responsibility for anyone or anything outside of themselves. They make themselves up as they go along. The antagonists of these novels are specific social forces no longer acceptable to the protagonist. The protest, however, is not a social one, but an entirely individual one. The writer gives emphasis to things, to the inanimate, which in the new fiction are more than symbols—they are almost characters. Important in *The Stranger* are the sun, the sea, the knife, the gun, the mother's coffin, and even the screws in the coffin. It is the force of the sun at the beginning of the novel that thrusts the protagonist into his crime and makes him fire so many shots at his victim.

This concern with the inanimate has become an obsession with writers influenced by the French existentialists and their successors, so that the trend is to deanimate the characters by giving them no names, to show their behavior in relation to objects such as chairs, tables, walls. Another trend is to eliminate plot. Since nothing ever does happen to a man, the writers claim, then nothing can happen to a character in a book. What men do, they say, is to sit around and stare at their thumbs or walk around and hit their shins on table legs. This is the way they must act in fiction. The result is frequently a kind of "coterie" writing art which is read only by other members of the in-group.

We can assume that writers today who cannot accept yesterday's fiction are in a transitional state. One reaction to living in a universe suddenly unlimited in size and power is to become smaller and smaller. We can expect, however, that once the size and the power have been accepted, the young writers will break through the restraints and create fiction worthy of the marvelous age. This is the challenge facing writers of the last decades of the twentieth century—writers who are learning to write today.

In the meantime, despite television, the public insists upon reading. Some have turned to nonfiction; others stay with the panoramic or horizontal novel which continues to be published. This is the novel that is considerably extended in time, space, characters, and scope of plot. The subject matter of the panoramic novel can be almost anything—social protest, sex, economic growth, war, politics—but the protagonist is going to be bigger than life, just as he has been since the times of Beowulf, the Cid, Roland, and Moses. He may be a union agitator, an artist, a boxer, or a businessman, but he will be an individual of stature and will overcome or be overcome by forces even bigger than himself.

Two examples of the panoramic novel in the United States are John Steinbeck's *The Grapes of Wrath* and Herman Melville's *Moby Dick*. Patrick White, the Australian winner of the 1973 Nobel Prize for literature, is a master of the panoramic novel.

Historical novels are likely to be panoramic in structure, since the time generally covers a long and important slice of history, such as an entire war or the colonization of a large land area. The conflicting characters of historical novels are invariably bigger than life—bigger than other men in size, spirit, courage, cruelty, and meanness. Examples of this kind of writing are *The Mask of Apollo* and *The King Must Die* by Mary Renault, *The World Is Not Enough* by Zoé Oldenbourg, *Rakossi* by Cecilia Holland, and *Exodus* by Leon Uris.

Biographical and autobiographical novels are panoramically or vertically conceived, depending on the time and scope the writer selects for his book. If the novel covers a lifetime, it is likely to spread out and include many characters; if it covers only a few significant days or weeks of the protagonist's life, it emerges as a vertical novel.

Science fiction, which has become increasingly important in fiction writing, may follow the vertical or the horizontal conception, again depending on the time and the scope. Suspense, mystery, adventure, and cowboy novels are inherently vertical novels as are the majority of original fiction paperbacks, whose themes are almost exclusively sex and violence.

Writers continue to follow the schools of writing they prefer: romanticism, realism, naturalism, expressionism, impressionism, symbolism. Thematically and structurally, the novelist is free. No subject is taboo, and no form, not even formlessness, is forbidden.

The Short-Story Writer

The short-story writer must determine early in his career what kind of story he wants to write and has the talent for writing. He must examine his own interests and taste. If he reads and enjoys commercial stories and believes in that kind of fiction, he will be able to write it, assuming, of course, that he has the talent and the willingness to learn his craft. If his interest lies in the literary magazine kind of story, he should develop his talent in that direction. If he is dissatisfied with both kinds and has original ideas of his own, he has a possible market in the small experimental magazines.

Occasionally a beginning writer decides to toss off a few slick or commercial stories, sell them, bank the money, then settle down to "serious" writing. He inevitably fails. *Cosmopolitan* does not buy his stories; he collects a stack of dusty, yellowing manuscripts and in despair, gives up the enormous pleasure of writing. He has confused slick or commercial writing with bad and insincere writing.

Actually, magazines and stories cannot be divided that simply, that specifically, into categories. For convenience, magazine publishers use the words "pulp," "slick," and "quality" to indicate the kind of stories they use. The pulp magazine, the confession, detective, or romance story magazine, is easily identified, but the slick and quality sometimes overlap. A so-called slick magazine like *Redbook* or *Cosmopolitan* often publishes quality stories, and a quality magazine like *Esquire* sometimes publishes slick stories.

The trend today in the slick magazines is toward quality in writing style and in the handling of the conflict or problem. The strictly formula story with its inevitably happy solution of the problem has been almost totally banished. This does not mean, however, that the quality story as the literary magazines see it is taking over the slick market. The taboos of subject matter remain the same, and the range of themes is still limited: family relationships, love, the triumph of virtue, and so on.

We may call the slick story "commercial" and the quality story "literary." *McCall's* and the *Ladies' Home Journal* are two of the family-type commercial magazines. *Playboy* and *Mademoiselle* are semicommercial. *Harper's, Atlantic Monthly,* and the ever-growing number of university reviews and quarterlies are literary magazines.

The commercial story is likely to be carefully plotted, with a well-established conflict leading to a definite climax. Surprise devices or tricks are used to carry the suspense, although the O. Henry trick ending is obsolete. The literary story may or may not have a plot. It may simply move forward to a climax that is only slightly higher than the rest of the story. The conflict is more subtly presented, and the problem may not be solved.

The characters in the commercial story are generally stock characters who seem real only because we have seen the stereotypes so many times. The literary writer is engaged with the inner workings of real people at a time of great stress. The reader identifies himself with these people at a subconscious or a secret level. The commercial heroine may be a typical secretary, a stereotype. The literary heroine may also be a secretary, but the writer is concerned with her uniqueness.

The commercial story is well written; the style is clear and smooth flowing, and the transitions are obvious. The dialogue is sharp and purposeful. The imagery may be clever, but it demands little of the reader. There is a sameness of style in most commercial stories. The style of the literary writer is clear but not obvious, and it cannot be confused with that of any other writer. William Faulkner's style is recognizable as his own; so is Katherine Mansfield's. Imagery, symbolism, and tone are important to the literary writer.

Subject matter or theme sharply separates commercial stories from literary ones. The commercial story must have a theme that will not alienate a body of readers. Readers can be alienated by references to politics or civil rights, attacks on institutions (the Church, the medical profession, the family), race problems, sexual perversions, and unpunished sin, such as adultery. Potential advertisers must never be offended by commercial stories. For example, you will never read about a drunken airline pilot in a commercial magazine, even though you read about him on page one of a newspaper. The themes of literary stories are unlimited. The writers will say that childhood isn't necessarily sacred but often a nightmare, that people beat their children and go unpunished, that evil can triumph, that homosexuality does exist, that an adulterer may never see the light, and that all that glitters is gold.

The Playwright

The potential playwright can easily identify himself. He is in love with the theater and woos it relentlessly. He doesn't read plays; he sees them. He knows what is going on. He is curious about the actors and actresses, about hits and misses in the theater, about developments in staging and directing. The young writer who has never been in a live theater but thinks he is going to be a playwright is like the story writer who submits stories to a defunct magazine.

The potential playwright has acquired a sense of total theater. He may be smitten with his own words, but he knows that they are only a part of the total production. He may bleed a little to see them cut or changed for the sake of the actor or some stage business, but he understands the need. He realizes that words, acting, staging, directing, producing, and an audience make the theater. A play is not a play until it is produced, heard, and seen.

In addition to his talent for words, the potential playwright has an ear for dialogue. He knows or learns the difference between conversation and dialogue. He has a sound sense of the dramatic and a feeling for pace. When he thinks about his characters, he hears them talk and sees them move across the stage. His eye is as sharp as his ear.

The writer who believes he can become a playwright, like fiction and nonfiction writers, may test himself with news events. Let him select seven news items that suggest drama or comedy to him and decide how he would handle them. Does he hear the people involved talking and moving on a stage or in a film? How much drama is suggested? Does the news event have the scope of a two-hour play or should it be limited to a half-hour one-act play? Does it necessarily cover so much territory and include so much action that it would adapt more naturally to the screen?

The playwright today needs courage and patience. The play as serious drama is in a state of transition; the showcases are expensive and limited, and the public's taste is unpredictable. During the past twenty years the number of serious plays produced on Broadway has lessened by exactly one-half, whereas the number of musicals and revues has doubled.

Although producers are making and remaking films of plays by older playwrights, it seems that Tennesee Williams, Arthur Miller, and Edward Albee have little more to say to the public today. It is also apparent that the theater of the absurd is unacceptable to the mass of theatergoers. It is the belief of several important groups interested in the theater that new playwrights must be encouraged and aided to produce the plays of the immediate future. These groups include the New Dramatists Committee, the Rockefeller

Foundation, the Ford Foundation, the Guggenheim Foundation, and the John Golden Fund.

Broadway's longtime inability to provide enough plays for theatergoers led to off-Broadway theater, which has also declined. Outside New York, lovers of the theater attend the ever-increasing number of small live theaters supported by communities, colleges, and universities. It is in these latter theaters that the young playwright must find his way.

The Television and Film Writer

Writers interested in the picture-length film and the teleplay should consider the limitations and obstacles in these fields. If they are not discouraged by the many handicaps, they will probably be successful. The market is certainly there.

First to be considered is the writer's need for an agent. About ninety-nine percent of the film and teleplay productions are handled by literary and talent agents. It is difficult to get an agent but not impossible. An ambitious agent will not refuse to handle an exceptional and marketable script.

In the movie industry there are three directions for a writer to take: the documentary film, the art film, and the commercial giant film (like *The Godfather*), which is the film industry's attempted answer to television. The documentary is nonfiction; the art film corresponds to quality fiction; the big and colorful films are slick and commercial.

The film-script writer can present his work in two ways: by story treatment or by a complete script. (Read chapter 7 on film and teleplay writing.)

The motion-picture film, like the novel or Broadway play, is virtually unlimited and unrestricted so far as subject matter, theme, and expression are concerned. It is somewhat more restricted structurally. As we shall see later, the writer of the art film is limited only by the camera.

The teleplaywright is faced by as many limitations and handicaps as the commercial short-story writer, although the need for teleplays is inexhaustible. His chief obstacles are time contrivances and subject matter. For the writer independent of the studios, the documentary, entertaining or educational, or both is the easiest approach to television.

The teleplaywright has a very small chance in serious drama unless he has an extraordinarily fresh dramatic idea, free from the taboos set up by producers, directors, distributors, advertisers, and other functionaries in the industry. In the drama field he may find success in the creation of a new series, presented in the form of a pilot script with story treatments of four or five additional scripts. Another possibility is the writing of a script episode for a running series.

Like the writers in all other fields, the teleplaywright must know what is going on. He must study the trends. If he decides to write a pilot script for a new series idea, he must make certain that the theme has not already been used and exhausted and that it is not against the trend. If he plans a script for a running series, he must be sure that the series hasn't been cancelled for the following season.

The writer's state of mind is important, too. If he rarely sees a televised show and thinks of his television set as a "boob tube," he will waste his time and talent trying to write for it. He must remember that he is writing not for the public but for the producers who believe, honestly enough, that they know what the public wants.

THE NONFICTION WRITER

Truth and facts in the second half of the twentieth century are more fascinating, more challenging than fiction; hence there is a growing demand for nonfiction while the fiction market shrinks. (The only increasing market in the world of fiction is that for science fiction and fantasy.)

The basic themes of nonfiction, oddly enough, have not changed. Perhaps they haven't changed since man first picked up a stone chisel and carved out symbols to describe the world around him. Leading all themes is the fight to survive. People want to read about this whether it concerns the survival of a man, a mouse, or a worm. The second most demanded theme is man's ability, in William Faulkner's words, not only to survive but to prevail. Another successful theme is how to prevail and to be happy at the same time. How to be and how to do are almost certain guarantees of a successful book or article: how to be beautiful, happy, popular, healthy, strong, successful (socially, sexually, professionally, spiritually) and how to do anything from subdividing a tiny planeria to visiting another planet. Still another popular theme is lifting the veil of mystery, going behind the scenes and observing how other people live, prevail, and die. Worlds other than man's own continuously challenge men's interest: the sea around him, the forests, the mountains, the rivers and lakes, and the inhabitants of these worlds. This accounts for the vast number of books on the natural sciences and the increasing number of television documentaries for the average man. Over the next hill is another basic theme. Hence the books, articles, and teleplays on the subject of travel.

A major factor in successful nonfiction writing is awareness of what is going on in the field, a perception of trends, an ability to distinguish between trends and fads, and a sense of the future. For example, during a presidential election year the reading public seizes upon anything having to do with dead or living presidents, their wives, their hobbies, and so on. After the election, except under extraordinary circumstances such as the assassination of President John F. Kennedy or the Watergate affair, the subject loses interest. The nonfiction writer must think ahead of the seasons if seasonal material is his subject. The writer who sends a Christmas article to a magazine publisher in November or December will receive a rejection slip, no matter how original or how well written his article may be. If he had sent it in June when the editor was making up his magazine, he might have sold it immediately. (Read appendix I on preparing and submitting manuscripts.)

The nonfiction writer who is writing books, literary or popular essays, or magazine articles must examine the nonfiction publications for a period of a year and ask himself where he will fit in, what he can offer that field.

He will notice that at the top of the list are autobiographies and biographies of great men or temporarily important ones in all areas of human activities. The list for one week may include such disparate subjects as Pancho Villa, Churchill, Lyndon Johnson, the Pope, and Queen Victoria. Only a little lower on the list are books about people whose fame is just as widespread but more ephemeral: stage and movie stars, artists, lesser royalty, traitors, spies. This list might include *Marilyn* by Norman Mailer. Historical figures never lose their appeal, and Abraham Lincoln is unique as a subject for books, studies, dramas, teleplays, political allusion, and even advertising slogans. Wars and the various aspects of sex are always popular subjects. The Kinsey Reports on sexual behavior were long-enduring, and more recently *Everything You Always Wanted to Know about Sex but Were Afraid to Ask* by Dr. David R. Reuben outsold all fiction. In the natural sciences Rachel Carson's *The Sense of Wonder, Silent Spring, The Edge of the Sea,* and *The Sea Around Us* have had enormous popular appeal. Jacques Cousteau's books about the sea are also of continuous interest.

Turning from books to magazines, the nonfiction writer recognizes famous names as authors of literary essays in literary magazines and popular essays in commercial and quality magazines. In commercial magazines he also finds authors of articles whose names he does not recognize.

For the beginning nonfiction writer the magazine article is a realistic beginning, and he will save time and temper by studying this market carefully. (Read chapter 12 on writing the magazine article.) He will see that the subjects of medicine, drugs, nutrition, beauty, and science are written by the magazine's staff or by authorities in these fields. And he will observe that there is no market for the little "think" pieces or editorials that young writers are fond of dashing off. He will notice, however, that here is an enormous market for subjects and ideas outside the few excluded ones handled by authorities.

He must be imaginative enough to realize that wherever he lives, in the city, woods, town, or country, he is surrounded by ideas for magazine articles. He must also realize that a magazine article is not a newspaper feature and that he may spend months completing the research for it. Like the fiction writer, he can find his ideas in newspaper reportage, but he cannot stop there, any more than the fiction writer can. While the fiction writer sits in his room and develops plot and theme, the article writer goes to the library and other places for source material.

His study of magazine needs over a period of a year will tell him how magazines change and how their handling of subjects change. For example, travel for travel's sake is no longer acceptable. A travel article needs a theme just as a story or essay does, and different magazines have different points of view about travel themes. *Travel & Leisure* likes sophisticated articles, whereas the automobile-club magazines (a good market for travel articles) emphasize the more practical aspects of traveling: mileage, costs, hotels, and so forth. Almost every writer knows at least one unforgettable character, but before he writes his profile, he should know how the magazines differ in their treatment of unforgettable characters.

As he sits in the library and reads the subjects of magazine articles, the nonfiction writer will learn, to his pleasure, that there is no subject in the world that is not repeatedly of interest to magazine publishers: occupations, peculiar and unpredictable; people who have conquered the unconquerable; problems of marriage and courtship; problems of child-raising, child-adoption, home environment; problems of the single man or woman, the stepfather, the divorced; man against society, against mountains, deserts, and seas; woman against time, against man; hobbies and avocations that have become vocations. The writer in the library learns another important fact: No magazine is all things to all people. By studying the magazines, he will learn the kind of articles the editors will accept for their specific readerships. Therefore, he will not waste his time sending an article that might interest the editors of *Esquire* or *Playboy* to a family-type magazine.

FICTION COMPARED WITH NONFICTION

The raw material of fiction and nonfiction most often comes from newspapers, news magazines, television, and other forms of communication, but it is raw. The writer's approach to events reported in these sources will usually determine whether he should write fiction or nonfiction.

Select seven news events that suggest possible stories to you. You will observe that as they appear in the newspaper, they are not stories but incidents or situations. They relate who did what when, where, and perhaps why. Missing are characterizations, focus, theme, point of view, the suspenseful use of time, and the details necessary for atmosphere.

Let us say that one of the news stories you selected is this one: A young girl selling cookbooks for a neighborhood project is enticed into a house by a young man who assures her that his uncle will buy one of the books. Inside the house she is attacked and raped by seven hoodlums who belong to a motorcycle club. Her father, a policeman, goes berserk at the police station when the hoodlums are arraigned. He shoots a young man who is being charged with a petty felony and had nothing to do with the attack on the policeman's daughter.

Here is all the raw material needed for fiction or nonfiction of varying lengths and quality. As it is, however, it is only a situation.

The short-story writer must decide whose story it is going to be: the girl's, the father's, a hoodlum's, perhaps the mother's. He must work out his characterizations, the conflict, the time or times, the setting, the immediate problem, the complications, the crises, and so on. He must find an ending for his story. When he has finished, his story may have little to do with the raw material read in the newspaper.

The nonfiction writer finds these things difficult, even impossible, to do. He is not concerned with story possibility, and it is likely that the seven newspaper reports he selected have no story potential. He is interested in the facts and in the sociological or political aspects of the story (juvenile delinquency, police brutality, narcotics usage) as his themes.

If ten writers in a group of twenty decide to create a story out of this news item, all ten will treat it differently, of course. One may write a pulp story for a true detective or a true confessions magazine, an "I Was a Teen-Age Hoodlum" kind of story. One may write a formula (or slick) story in which the problem will be solved to almost everybody's satisfaction. A romance will be added. The girl will not be raped; her father or mother or one of the hoodlums will rescue her. Another kind of writer will create a quality story, emphasizing some psychological aspect of the situation. Perhaps he will show how an entire family can be destroyed by a seemingly meaningless act.

Some writers may see in the situation the scope of a novel, a three-act play, or an hour-length teleplay. Someone may see how it would fit into a television series.

The situation is not new; few situations are. The success of the author will depend upon his making it seem new, fresh, and engrossing.

The other ten writers in the group may decide to create a piece of nonfiction out of the idea, a magazine article or even a book on the subject of juvenile delinquency, family life, motorcycle clubs, police brutality. Their problem will be to find a new angle on one of these subjects.

The writer who in defense of a poorly structured story says, "But this is the way he was, and this is the way it happened," should be writing nonfiction, not fiction. He will cling to a characterization of his grandfather because that was the way the old man behaved. Any other representation to this writer would seem betrayal.

The fiction writer, however, knows that it isn't important for a character to be real or to be portrayed exactly the way he is. He must seem real. The fiction writer knows that events seldom occur as related in unified stories, but rather as a sequence of incidents. He will distort characterizations as well as events and incidents to make his story. There is doubtless a story in every man's life, but his life has to be adapted to the story, not the story to his life.

The fiction and the nonfiction writer have much in common. They both must have a sense of drama or the dramatic and a knowledge of structure. Like the story, the magazine article must move toward a climax and produce a single effect. Both writers work with a theme, a conflict, or a problem; both have developed or are developing their particular style.

The background of the nonfiction writer is likely to be different from the fiction writer's. He needs more formal education or a background of experience in painstaking research; he must know where to go to find essential information. He has to have a sincere respect for facts and for the truth that is not necessary for the fiction writer, who is concerned only with making something seem true. If the nonfiction writer is going to write about living people, he must learn the delicate, intricate, difficult art of interviewing. He must be passionately concerned with details. He has to write with authority; in fact, he must be an authority. And, generally speaking, he must be a specialist.

He has some advantages over the fiction writer. The trend in magazines and books today is away from fiction into the territory of nonfiction. Magazine publishers now use more articles than stories, and book publishers are more inclined to gamble on non-fiction than on fiction. Nonfiction, depending upon its timeliness, lasts much longer on better-seller lists than fiction. Inspirational and how-to nonfiction books have proved to be the most enduring in public taste. The Bible leads, followed closely by *The Prophet*. Other long-continuing best sellers include books on marriage problems, sex, business and social success, collections of poetry, and single volumes of poetry such as *The Rubáiyát* of Omar Khayyám. It is significant that *Robinson Crusoe*, a how-to kind of novel, and *Uncle Tom's Cabin*, an impassioned sociological tract, are among the top ten of the all-time best-selling novels.

The fiction writer has his advantages, too. He enjoys a feeling of total creation. His imagination is unbounded, and he can engage the reader, whatever his subject matter may be.

3

Material for Fiction

> *It is necessary to remember and necessary to forget, but it is better for a writer to remember. It is necessary for him to live purposely, which is to say: to live and to remember having done so.*

With these words William Saroyan tells us what writers have to write about: what they remember from what they have perceived.

PERCEPTION AND REMEMBRANCE

The story is everywhere, and every writer has his own way of looking for it. Some writers, like Hemingway, traveled to find it; others, like Eudora Welty, found it by staying in a small town. Some writers are rooted; others drift. Some need the whole world; others can find a dozen stories in a single block of their hometown. Katherine Anne Porter did not like groups of writers; other writers function best within a group. But wherever they are, it is safe to say that they are reacting, responding, and remembering.

Some critics state categorically that if a writer is afraid he has nothing to write about, he should simply give up writing and do something else. Such a generalization would eliminate many a talented but timid beginner who feels that all the stories have been told which, to be sure, is true. It is only from what the in-

21

dividual writer has perceived and remembered that his own story variation can emerge.

I sometimes offer this as a possible assignment to beginning writers:

Develop the following situation into a complete story idea: A young married couple of average income in Washington, D.C., are invited to a party where they will meet many important and interesting people. The woman feels that this marks a turn for the better in their meager social life. Her immediate problem is how to make an impressive appearance with her limited wardrobe.

Some of the student-writers select another assignment, for nothing in this situation stirs their memories. Others are moved to develop a complete story outline. One or two may write an entire story. None of the stories will have any resemblance to the others, for the characters, the setting, the theme, the feeling all come from the writers' own perceptions and memories. Certainly their story plans and completed stories will in no way resemble what Maupassant, through his perception and memory, created as "The Necklace."

Subject matter comes from perception (seeing, hearing, smelling, tasting, touching) that is stored away in the memory to be pulled out later by the imagination and stirred and blended into a new creative form.

Katherine Anne Porter showed the importance of perception and memory to the writer in her discussion of source material for her novelette *Noon Wine*. Her memory went back as far as her third year to bring out people, situations, objects, and feelings to merge with later memories and thus to create this excellent story.

Perception does dull, but the writer cannot allow his to dull, any more than the painter can let his paints dry up. For this is what the writer has. Perhaps basically this is what a writer is: a person whose perception has not dulled.

Children, of course, perceive. The baby struggles constantly to see, to hear, to touch. This is why one's earliest sense memories may be stronger than those of only a year ago. It is easy to remember what the snows of childhood smelled and tasted and felt like, while forgetting those of last winter.

The senses dull with age in defense against the batter and clatter of sounds and sights, but the writer has to remain a child. He has to look and listen as if for the first time. If his perception has dulled, it has to be sharpened.

Aldous Huxley wrote about D. H. Lawrence's ability to see the world anew.

> He looked at things with the eyes, so it seemed, of a man who had been at the brink of death and to whom, as he emerges from the darkness, the world reveals itself as unfathomably beautiful and mysterious. For Lawrence, existence was one continuous convalescence; it was as though he were newly reborn from a mortal illness every day of his life. What these convalescent eyes saw, his most casual speech would reveal. A walk with him in the country was a walk through that marvelously rich and significant landscape which is at once the background and principal personage of all his novels.*

A useful practice for the writer is to stop, listen to, and to try to put into words the many sounds he has been taking for granted or trying to eliminate. The sounds on a traffic-busy freeway are not like any other sounds, nor are they the same to any two writers. Writer A hears ocean sounds differently from writer B. Ocean and traffic sounds in the middle of the night are not the same as those in the morning. Every tree has its specific sound; so do the different kinds of rain. The writer asks himself: How do these sound in words? What are the sounds of cold and heat? And what do cold and heat look like?

It is important for the writer to see the world around him and record it for his later use. If he purposely looks at a tree—a eucalyptus, a jacaranda, a palm tree, a birch, a maple—he will sense things about it he had never suspected. It will suggest images and symbols to him; it will recall other sense memories, other connotations. What does a cloud actually look like? A rock? If he looks at a coastline as if for the first time, he will see wave patterns he had never noticed. If he spends a half-hour looking at the blossom of a passionflower vine, he will be able to write two pages about it.

As he sharpens his perception, the writer will notice the im-

* Aldous Huxley, *The Art of Seeing* (New York: Harper & Row, 1942).

portance, too, of his senses of smell and touch. He will notice that his sense of smell, assaulted as it constantly is, has almost vanished, that the remembered smells go back to his childhood rather than to yesterday or this morning. He will find that although his sense of touch may not have dulled, he has neglected to use it and to remember what he has perceived through it. His fingers must learn again what things feel like: the differences in the feel of salt water and fresh water, of tree barks, rocks, soil, and other materials.

The writer will find endless excitement in the sharpening of his senses in places such as a flower or vegetable market, a courtroom, an elevator, a cafeteria or a bar, a street corner or a bus station, a crowded or a neglected beach, or the top of a mountain.

CHOICE OF SUBJECT

Subject matter is necessarily autobiographical in part, and some writers find in themselves inexhaustible source material for fiction. Others may find inspiration for one entire novel or only a story or two in themselves. John Cheever said that he was unable to write about himself at all, that his perceptions were altogether of other people.

It can be observed that sooner or later almost every writer must get out of his system a story the theme of which is the end of his own innocence—the day his childhood ended and he stepped, jumped, or was pushed into manhood. Many variations on this theme have been composed, all of them different in characterization, style, and plot.

Katherine Mansfield, in "The Garden Party," used this theme so quietly, so subtly, it almost seems not to be a story. But it is a young girl's first step into womanhood, her first venture into a world beyond the blissful world of her childhood, and her first experience with death.

If the writer is going to use his own end of innocence as a story theme and write it as if it had never been done before, he must study himself, understand his feelings about himself, establish his own identity. Who is he? What does he look like to himself, to people who love him, to people who hate him? What does he look and sound like to his Creator? What is his own dominant trait, his own distinguishing characteristic, his motivating force?

While he is investigating himself, he may learn that although the end of his innocence does not challenge him as story material, some other period in his life is clearly a drama. Many people have said that there is at least one story or drama in every man's life, and I strongly believe this to be true. In every person's life there is surely a turning time, a moment, a day, a week, or a month that has made a difference in his life, that has mattered. And this is story material, its scope and significance depending on the sharpness, quality, and interest of the thing that has mattered and the person to whom it has mattered.

The protagonist of J. D. Salinger's story "For Esmé—With Love and Squalor" is a sergeant in World War II, but the important time for him during all those war years was the time of his friendship with two children—important because of their effect on the rest of his life.

For my own novel, *The Nine Days of Father Serra*, I selected what to me were the most significant days in the life of a man to whom all days were significant. These were the nine days that tested the man's own faith and that of his companions, that kept the Spaniards in California, that discouraged the Russians from settling south of the Russian River in Northern California, that actually determined the course of American history in the West. These few days mattered more than the time he spent building missions and achieving other kinds of success.

These moments of dramatic decision and dramatic happenings may be clearly seen in the lives of people important in history. The drama of Judas is his moment of betrayal, of Christ is his Crucifixion. Rarely is the death of a man the greatest drama of his life. Dramatic as was the death of Lincoln, the stories, novels, plays, and poetry written about him deal not with his death but with momentous times of his life. When men seem to die too soon (for example, Presidents Roosevelt and Kennedy), their deaths have dramatic impact and may be considered the momentous times. Or when death is the only dramatic event in someone's life, the life of the family of "A Good Man Is Hard to Find," for example, then it is the mattering moment. The important time of Napoleon's life was the Battle of Waterloo. With President Truman, we can assume that the dramatic moment of his life was the moment of his decision to use the atom bomb against the Japanese. The most dramatic moments of President Eisenhower's life were surely before he became president.

A writer may not see the time that matters in himself, but he may recognize it in others, in his father, mother, friend, or even a stranger. When he has selected, modified, and arranged the elements of his story, it will probably not be recognizable, but the drama will have been born out of one of those significant times.

Start Writing!

1. Fiction comes from experience, continuously. What did you do, see, hear, or in some other way experience today that might develop into a story?
2. William Burroughs says, "There is only one thing a writer can write about: what is before his senses at the moment of writing." Do this. Find your scene, your experience. Examine it with your senses rather than with your mind. Does a story come to you? If so, write it immediately.
3. Many ordinary happenings are situations that suggest possible stories. Following are four such situations:
   A fat and sweating father is playing baseball with his nine-year-old son. The boy would like to be playing with his friends or watching television. Show what is going on in the minds of these two people.
   On Halloween night, an elderly woman mistakes two hoodlums for kids on a trick-or-treat call (or vice versa).
   A prostitute passes a garden where a small blind boy is playing. She knows he is her son. Could you develop this story without sentimentality?
   The scene is the visitors' room in a mental hospital. Two brothers (or sisters) are talking. At the end of the visit, the

brother whose conversation seemed unintelligent and without meaning is seen to be the visitor, not the patient.

4. Almost everyone you know has a story in him. It is likely to originate in the person's most crucial, most important time, perhaps a month, a week, an hour, or a few minutes. Consider from this point of view five people you know. Do they suggest five possible stories?

5. Much literature has been written around this particular theme: Early in life most people realize, perhaps suddenly, perhaps gradually, that this is not the best of all possible worlds and isn't going to be. Does this suggest a story?

4

The Anatomy of a Short Story

The short story, like any other piece of writing from a James Joyce novel to a one-line ad, starts somewhere, goes somewhere, and ends somewhere. It may come to a dead end, but the important thing is that it does go somewhere.

The short-story writer has a purpose: to take a character or characters from one place to another. The journey may be a rough one, but the character (the protagonist) and the reader will know that they have made the journey, that something has happened to both of them.

The writer must have a fairly clear idea of what direction the story will take and where it will end. He will, of course, allow it to take unexpected twists and turns, giving it all the freedom it needs, so long as it comes back and inches, walks, runs, or plunges toward the original destination.

The planning of the short story can begin anywhere, depending upon the preferences and compulsions of the individual writer. Some writers begin with a character; others, with a situation or plot; still others evolve a story from a theme that interests them. We may assume that William Faulkner created "A Rose for Emily" out of a character rather than from a situation or a theme. Flannery O'Connor may have conceived "A Good Man Is Hard to Find" from the character of the grandmother or from a situation she might have read about in a newspaper. D. H. Lawrence may have developed his story "The Rocking Horse Winner" from its theme, a sense of values.

As soon as a writer has his story beginning, he plans his ending. Writers who say they just sit down and write, not knowing where the story will go, generally find themselves with a story that goes nowhere, especially not into a magazine. Everything that goes into the story has to lead inevitably, though unpredictably, to the end.

SETTING

Within the brief scope of the short story, the writer has much to accomplish from the very start. First he establishes the where and the when, or the setting. Setting for its own sake has little meaning, but as a part of atmosphere, character revelation, and plot development, it is extremely important. The tendency of the beginning writer is to make his place descriptions separate from the story itself; this was a popular device in the leisurely literature of the nineteenth century. Today the setting description is expected to be an organic part of the story, useful only when the character or the tone of the story is affected by it. Also, the setting may be implicitly rather than explicitly expressed. For example, the setting of Flannery O'Connor's "A Good Man Is Hard to Find" is revealed through dialogue.

Faulkner, in "A Rose for Emily," describes through his narrator the house where most of the story takes place. The description is explicit and detailed, for the house is as important to the story as the characters. In the first three paragraphs the setting is established: The description of the house shows that it had been built in the seventies in the select part of a Southern town but is now part of a dilapidated neighborhood. The time is established: The story begins in the present time, but the third paragraph indicates that it will go back to 1894. Words used in the first three paragraphs also suggest the tone or atmosphere of the story: died, funeral, decay, cemetery, graves, and so on.

CHARACTERS

At the very start of the story, the characters must be introduced, mentioned, or implied. Faulkner presented his protagonist, his antagonist, and a minor character in the first sentence of his story:

> When Miss Emily Grierson died, our whole town went to her funeral: the men through a sort of respectful affection for a fallen monument, the women most out of curiosity to see the inside of her house, which no one save an old manservant—a combined gardener and cook—had seen in at least ten years.

By the end of the third paragraph all the characters except one have appeared, and their dominant traits have been revealed.

Some writers do not describe their characters physically, because the physical description is not vital to the story. Faulkner, however, through his narrator, describes the physical appearance of Miss Emily at different time periods, for it is organic to the story. The sixth paragraph describes her appearance at the turn of the century:

> . . . a small, fat woman in black, with a thin gold chain descending to her waist and vanishing into her belt, leaning on an ebony cane with a tarnished gold head. Her skeleton was small and spare; perhaps that was why what would have been merely plumpness in another was obesity in her. She looked bloated, like a body long submerged in motionless water, and of that pallid hue. Her eyes, lost in the fatty ridges of her face, looked like two pieces of coal pressed into a lump of dough. . . .

Later in the story there will be descriptions of Miss Emily when she was young, when she was middle-aged, and when she died— all of them significant in the story development. The other characters emerge as real people, but their traits and behavior are limited to those which affect the protagonist.

STRUCTURE

At the beginning of the story the writer must also indicate or imply the theme and the problem or the conflict. He has to show the purpose of the story and what it is about. The first paragraphs of the Faulkner story imply that it is going to be concerned with the theme of the outsider, a victim of her time and place, of the effect of Southern traditions upon a person born too late for them. The beginning of the story also suggests a conflict between Miss Emily and the town, between the forces each represents. The insiders are going to be the town, her father, and even her Yankee lover, who at least had a function in the town.

Another element to be established at the beginning of a story is the point of view. The point of view in Faulkner's story is an unusual one, that of the first-person plural narrator. "When Miss Emily Grierson died, *our* whole town went to the funeral." We, the town, will tell the story from our point of view. This point of view is useful, for it gives the narrator great freedom in moving back and forth in time and enables him to present Miss Emily through the eyes of the whole community. It limits him in that he cannot enter anybody's mind but his own. It is clear, too, from the beginning, that the focus is going to be on Miss Emily.

The initial or immediate problem of any story is a minor one that upsets the status quo or demands a change from the status quo. The initial problem of Faulkner's story is the unsuccessful attempt by the city fathers to collect property taxes from Miss Emily. This, too, is a part of the very beginning of a story.

The writer, before the story really starts to move, has thus told whom and what the story is about, where and when it is taking place; he has at least implied what the main conflict is; he has established the tone or atmosphere; and he has initiated the immediate problem.

In most plotted stories the road, as it continues, rises, moving from crisis to crisis and finally to climax. From there it may drop a little. In other kinds of stories the road may move in a flat line and rise slightly at the end, if at all.

"A Rose for Emily" is a plotted story, even though the structure (the anatomy) is concealed. The transition is made from the initial problem to the first crisis, which, oddly enough, takes place thirty years before the initial problem. "So she vanquished them, horse and foot, just as she had vanquished them thirty years before about the smell. That was two years after her father's death and a short time after her sweetheart had deserted her, too."

The transition prepares the ground for the first crisis, her father's death, and the second crisis, her hopeless love affair with the Yankee construction man. The story continues its climb until Miss Emily's purchase of the rat poison and her lover's disappearance. The story begins to fall at this point, to reach a second and shocking climax in the last line.

Faulkner maintains suspense throughout the story even though the reader knows what the narrator does not, namely that Miss Emily poisoned her lover and had kept his body in the house all these years. The reader does not expect the final climax, yet is able to accept it.

The distinguished quality in the anatomy of this story is Faulkner's use of periods of time. Generally speaking, the short story takes place in the least possible time, an hour, a day, or at most a week. This story covers most of a woman's lifetime, from her youth to her old age. Nor does the writer handle time chronologically. He selects the periods of time in her life that build the story up logically.

At the end of the story, the reader will feel the single effect that every successful story must make, the single effect or perhaps the revelation that results when the focus of the story is sharp, the characters believable yet interesting, the point of view steady, all the parts well balanced, and when, most important of all, there hangs over the story a kind of mist or an aura, the magic that is peculiarly the writer's own and makes it possible for the reader to say, "Only Faulkner could have written that story."

INTRODUCTION

The introduction of a well-constructed short story will include the setting, the major character, the theme or its implication, and a hint of the immediate problem. That is, the introduction will engage the interest of the reader.

Start Writing!

1. Write a paragraph in which the tone or atmosphere indicates that the story is going to be a tragic one.
2. Introduce a protagonist by showing him watching a football game in the stadium of his university.
3. Write a page of dialogue that would indicate the theme is one of bitter jealousy.
4. Write the introduction of the story as a scene of action, presenting an immediate problem or conflict.

CRISES AND CLIMAX

Start Writing!

In the following suggested plots for short stories, write a one-page synopsis, developing the story through one or two crises and a climax.

1. A married man in his late 30s goes to a resort alone and out of boredom and vanity, picks up a married woman (something he has done before). They spend two nights together; then they return to their homes and spouses. She has not been gone a week when he realizes that he loves her completely and forever.
2. They were a devoted couple for years, yet when her mother died and she was free to marry him their relationship suddenly came to an end.
3. When the promotion went through and he had every reason to expect that there would be another within seven or eight months, he began to drink heavily; then he deserted his wife and children and lived for a time with another woman in a shabby downtown hotel. Now he has left town, and as far as his family and former employers know, he is gone for good.
4. Nobody liked her, and really, there were any number of good reasons. Yet when she suddenly died a number of people felt a deep sense of loss.
5. A woman discovers that becoming successful in her work has

made her unable to tolerate her husband. There are children involved and strong ties between their families.

Suggested Reading

William Faulkner, "A Rose for Emily," from *Collected Short Stories of William Faulkner*. (New York: Random House, 1957).

Flannery O'Connor, "A Good Man Is Hard to Find," from *Short Stories of Flannery O'Connor*. (New York: Harcourt Brace Jovanovich, 1955).

5

The Novel and the Novelette

Structurally, the novel and the short story have in common the need for a consistent point of view, clear focus, a direction or sense of flow toward something, a problem or conflict, crises leading to a climax, and some kind of resolution. Both, of course, need a theme.

THE NOVEL

The obvious difference between a novel and a short story is length, but the beginning writer must realize that length does not result from mere word mileage but from the scope of the idea. Some ideas will support a short story, but will not hold up a novel; the novel will be thin and verbose. The story idea of O'Connor's "A Good Man Is Hard to Find" could scarcely have been developed into a novel idea, and the novel idea of F. Scott Fitzgerald's *Tender Is the Night* could not possibly have been contained in a short story. The first question the beginning novelist must ask himself is: Do I have an idea that will support a novel?

The chief difference between the short story and the novel is the desired effect. Whereas in the short story the writer seeks a compelling single effect, the novelist works toward a comprehensive unified effect. To obtain his single effect, the short-story writer involves an individual in conflict with another person, with himself, or with an idea. The novelist, for his unified effect, sets up his character against life or a segment of life itself. The grand-mother in "A Good Man Is Hard to Find" is in conflict with her own nature. The protagonist of *Tender Is the Night* is portrayed in relationship with his total world.

Once he has judged his subject matter to have the scope of a novel, the writer is fairly free as far as form is concerned. What matters is a sense of flow. The writer may use flashbacks and stream-of-consciousness technique, but he cannot allow his novel to become static. It may flow slowly, but it must flow.

Structure

The point of view must be consistent, but this does not mean that it cannot be changed within the novel. Faulkner, for example, divided his *The Sound and the Fury* into four sections, relating each section from the point of view of a different person. However, inside each section the point of view is consistent. Some novelists use the same point of view throughout their books, while others may use Faulkner's technique. Occasionally a writer will alternate the point of view, chapter by chapter or section by section. In long novels writers usually use the omniscient point of view which enables them to enter the minds of as many characters as they please.

Fitzgerald used the author-omniscient point of view to tell the story of *Tender Is the Night*, but he changed the focus. The focus, or the camera, in the first part of the book is placed on Rosemary, the eighteen-year-old Hollywood star. The second and longer part of the novel is focused on Richard Diver and his wife, with Rose-mary entering only occasionally. The unified effect at the end is achieved through the disintegration of Richard Diver, with Rose-mary almost forgotten. The writer must carefully control his focus and avoid being carried away by his interest in a minor character. The focus of *The Sound and the Fury*, despite the four points of view, is on one person, Candy. Even in a novel as long and as peopled as *Gone With the Wind*, the focus invariably returns to the two protagonists.

The theme of a novel, which must be implied or at least hinted at from the very beginning, is likely to be more general, more comprehensive, than that of the short story, and the novel is not necessarily limited to one theme. The basic theme of most novels is concerned with the flaw in a human being that makes it impossible for him to handle life as he encounters it. Or the theme may be how, in spite of his flaw, the human being can stand up to whatever life hands him. There are, of course, many variations on this broad theme.

The overall theme of *Tender Is the Night* is a man's disintegration caused by an unconquerable flaw in his character. The story is about a brilliant psychiatrist who falls in love with one of his patients, and urged by her relatives, marries her. His gradual disintegration is the result of his easy, comfortable, and pleasurable life with a very rich woman.

The novel may involve several conflicts in contrast to the single one of the short story. The main conflicts of the Fitzgerald novel are those of Dr. Richard Diver with himself and with his wife. But there are others: between the doctor and Rosemary, the Hollywood actress, between the doctor and several minor characters, and between the minor characters.

In a novel time may be used in a loose way that is not possible in most short stories. A novel may cover the span of several generations, or in a novel like James Joyce's *Ulysses*, the "playing time" may be only a day. The time span of *Tender Is the Night* is the total adulthood of Dr. Diver.

Fitzgerald did not use his time chronologically but in flashbacks that logically build up his story from crisis to crisis. This novel begins at a significant time in Dr. Diver's life, just before his decadence becomes visible. The first third of the book takes place at this time. The second division of the book begins in Diver's twenty-sixth year, in 1917, when as a brilliant medical graduate he is considered too important to be sent to the war and is working in Zurich. This division carries the story through his love affair with Nicole, his patient; their marriage; the birth of their children; and their life together until the time of page one of the book. The story then continues chronologically as Diver is completely defeated and accepts the defeat by his wife (the climax). A short denouement, covering several years, shows Diver's return to America and his several unsuccessful attempts to open a doctor's office.

It is important for the beginning writer to notice that if Fitzgerald had told his story chronologically the crisis would not have risen in intensity all the way to the climax. Using the long flashback, he was able to present his crises according to their intensity: first, Diver's love affair with Rosemary, which does not seem very important; second, the revelation that Nicole is insane; third, Diver's decision against his own judgment to marry an insane woman, who as a little girl had been seduced by her father; fourth, events leading to the loss of his clinic; and finally, his acceptance of the loss of his wife and children.

Another difference between the short story and the novel is the leisurely introduction in the novel of the important elements of a story. Whereas the first one or two paragraphs of a story must include or imply these elements, the novelist may use a chapter or two to introduce them. The first six thousand words of *Tender Is the Night*, or what would ordinarily be a chapter, show the point of view, author omniscient; the setting, the French Riviera; the characters: Rosemary and her mother, the in-group (most of the minor characters) on the beach, dominated by Richard Diver and his wife; the possible theme, the life of the self-exiled, pampered rich; the immediate problem, Rosemary's falling in love with Diver; and an element of suspense, the suspicion that something is wrong with the seemingly perfect Divers.

It is easy enough to look at the structure of a novel written by someone else. The important thing is to handle one's own skillfully.

Plan

One method of planning the novel is to write a fairly complete synopsis of the story and some detailed descriptions of the important people. From the synopsis the writer can then outline his chapters, at least four or five, if not all of them. The outlines will include the story to be developed and an indication of the dialogue. From the outlines he can then write his complete chapters. The important thing is not to allow the synopsis or the outlines to be too rigid. It is possible that when the author has written four or five chapters, he will see that as the characters have been developed or revealed they should take another course altogether. He should not be bound by his original plan, but he must be aware of his ultimate destination.

The writer will also save frustration and trouble by writing out his novel in scenes, by showing what is going on, what is happening to whom, and who is talking. In this way he can avoid the expository kind of writing that can be fatal to any narrative. His people are doing something; he is not explaining what they are doing.

The beginning writer cannot sit down and just start writing with the wistful hope that "the story will write itself" or that "the characters will write it for him." They won't. He has, therefore, two sins to avoid: rigidity and vagueness.

THE NOVELETTE

The novelette, structurally, is neither a short novel nor a long short story. It does have the single effect characteristic of the short story rather than the unified effect of the novel, but the time span is less limited, and there is room for more rounded minor characters than there is in the short story.

Particularly successful as novelettes are Faulkner's "The Bear," Hemingway's "The Old Man and the Sea," Orwell's "Animal Farm," and Katherine Anne Porter's "Old Mortality," a companion to her *Pale Horse, Pale Rider* and *Noon Wine*.

The theme of "Old Mortality" is concerned with tradition and youth; the single effect comes off at the end with Miranda's words to herself:

> Her mind closed stubbornly against remembering, not the past but the legend of the past, other people's memory of the past, at which she had spent her life peering in wonder. . . . I don't want any promises, I won't have false hopes . . . I can't live in their world any longer, she told herself. . . . Let them tell their stories to each other. Let them go on explaining how things happened. I don't care. At least I can know the truth about what happens to me, she assured herself silently, making a promise to herself, in her hopefulness, her ignorance.

The point of view of "Old Mortality" is that of two girls, Maria and Miranda, though finally it is exclusively Miranda's. The focus remains for the most part on the extraordinarily beautiful Aunt Amy, whose story and character are gradually revealed to Miranda through other characters. The focus falls on Uncle Gabriel, Aunt Amy's antagonist. There is nothing in the story that does not contribute to Miranda's understanding of Aunt Amy and Uncle Gabriel. Hence, the sharp single effect of the total story. The story of Aunt Amy would have no meaning at all except in relationship to Miranda.

Mrs. Porter told her story chronologically and in three time periods: 1885–1902, 1904, and 1912, paralleling the revelation of Aunt Amy to the growing up of Miranda, Miranda's elopement, her return for Uncle Gabriel's funeral, and her decision (the climax) to escape again from both her home and her husband, from anything that "threatened to forbid her making her own discoveries."

The Anatomy of Long Fiction

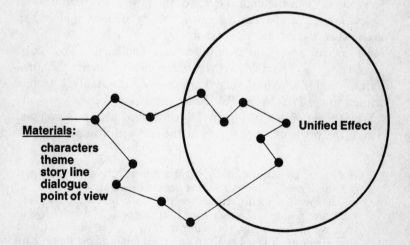

Materials:
  characters
  theme
  story line
  dialogue
  point of view

Unified Effect

The success of long works depends upon the skill with which the writer provides a unified effect. In a novel the size of *Dr. Zhivago* the effect consists of a variety of influences contributing to a unified experience for the reader.

The diagram above shows how the materials of a work lead to a unified effect in a novel or novelette.

Start Writing!

Select a novel or novelette and show how the materials all lead to a unified effect.

Suggested Reading

William Faulkner, "The Bear," from *Go Down, Moses.* (New York: Random House, 1942).

F. Scott Fitzgerald, *Tender Is the Night.* (New York: Scribner, 1933).

Katherine Anne Porter, "Old Mortality," from *Pale Horse, Pale Rider.* (New York: Harcourt Brace Jovanovich, 1939).

6

Science Fiction and Fantasy

Man's rapid projection into space in the direction of other possible worlds has given impetus to science fiction, making it a fast-growing literary form.

There are two basic types: science fiction proper based on scientific possibilities and science fantasy in which the writer may deal as he pleases with scientific impossibilities or improbabilities. The only requirement is dramatic credibility. George Orwell's *1984* is an example of the first type; *The Martian Chronicles* by Ray Bradbury illustrates the second type. The two types may, of course, be combined.

The writer should first acquaint himself with the anthologies of science-fiction short stories, novels, and the forty to fifty magazines that publish only science fiction and fantasy. Although the first science-fiction anthology, *Amazing Stories Annual*, was published in 1927, it was not until the 1950s that publishers saw the commercial value of such collections. In fact, science fiction as a form in itself was not recognized until the Library of Congress established a distinct science-fiction heading in its 1950–1954 listing of Books: Subjects. In 1971 the American Library Association published a Science Fiction Story Index; containing 3,400 titles, it consists of an author-title index, a bibliography of indexed anthologies, and a title-author and anthology-code index. This is an excellent reference book for the subject matter. Even more useful are the two volumes *The Greatest Science Fiction Stories of All Time* and *The Greatest Science Fiction Novellas of All Time.* These are stories chosen by the members of the Science Fiction Writers of America, edited by Ben Bova, and published by Doubleday. The writer who would like a comprehensive picture of science fiction today and its future course should have a copy of *Science Fiction; Today and Tomorrow* edited by Reginald Bretnor and published by Harper & Row, 1974.

The subject matter of science fiction includes space, the exploration of other worlds, meetings with other forms of life, travel into the future or into the past, and changes brought about in people through science either destructively or constructively. There are hundreds of variations, too, on these major topics.

The history of science fiction and fantasy in literature goes back to the olden times when its themes were used as vehicles for social comment, for example, the ideas expressed by Aesop's talking animals. These themes were based on what was manifestly impossible. True science fiction progressed with science itself and was based on what could some day happen. Jules Verne and H. G. Wells were the fathers of true science fiction, and much of what they wrote not only could but did happen. Advances in nuclear power and allied subjects opened up a vast field for science-fiction writers, and the end of World War II marked the beginning and the flourishing of many science-fiction and fantasy magazines. Achievements in space by the scientists and astronauts in the late sixties and early seventies have given enormous impetus to interest in science fiction. A study of the previously mentioned reference books shows a growing interest by editors of general magazines on science fiction and fantasy.

It is important for the science-fiction writer to remember that his subject matter does not permit him to deviate to any extent from literary tradition. The single or unified effect must be accomplished. Characters must be developed as fully and as realistically as if they peopled any other fictional story, play, or novel. The plot structure must make sense. Tone, atmosphere, and style are also important. Conflicts and problems must be clearly apparent from the beginning, and the element of suspense must follow the story to its end. The most important literary factor for the science-fiction writer to keep in mind is theme. It is not enough for the writer to tell merely what happens next without engaging the reader in some underlying meaning or theme.

THE SCIENCE-FICTION NOVEL

C. S. Lewis, a professor of medieval literature at Cambridge until his death in 1963 and a writer of theological books, was also a respected science-fiction writer. The serious science-fiction writer should study Lewis's famous space trilogy, *Out of the Silent Planet*, *Perelandra*, and *That Hideous Strength*, as an example of quality booklength science fantasy.

Another trilogy of importance to the science-fiction writer is the *Lord of the Rings* by J. R. R. Tolkien, who created and immortalized the hobbits. These books, which in 1974 had gone through 47 printings, have the structure of the long panoramic novel. The story of the prolonged struggle to possess and control the celebrated One Ring rises in climactic excitement all the way to the end of the third volume when the Third Age of Middle Earth comes to a close and the unpredictable Age of the Dominion of Man begins. Structurally, these novels follow the plan that has engaged readers for thousands of years: The hero is offered an opportunity for the Great Adventure. He accepts the challenge and crosses the barrier between the ordinary world and the world of adventure. He slays the preliminary dragons and goes his way, overcoming the obstacles that come between him and what he is searching for. This general structure is as old as Moses's search for the promised land, and there is no evidence that the reading public will ever lose interest in it.

In addition to following the structural plan that readers have always demanded, these novelists present characters with whom the readers can identify as well as characters whom they hate and fear.

THE SCIENCE-FICTION SHORT STORY

An outstanding fantasist in short fiction today is Ray Bradbury, whose quality is attributable partly to his use of a theme in addition to an out-of-the-ordinary story, partly to his characters, who might be you, I, or Ray Bradbury. For subject matter Bradbury selects the macabre, the awesome, the terrifying. He writes of love, loneliness, revenge, and atonement against a background in the world of fantasy. Once the reader accepts Bradbury's impossible, he willingly accepts the probability or credibility that follows.

Ray Bradbury's success in the general writing field today may be attributed to his craftsmanship. He has mastered the technique of fiction, knowing that fantasy alone will not carry a story. A study of his short-story collection, *Twice Twenty-Two*, will profit the beginning science-fiction writer.

Dr. Isaac Asimov, author of about 150 novels and collections of short stories, merits close study. However bizarre the setting and the plot may be, his characters are human beings, expressing the various human passions and occasionally a sense of humor.

Robert Heinlein, a longtime favorite of science-fiction readers, is especially adept at the technological story which is often referred to as "hard-core" science fiction. He may be studied profitably for his ability to structure a story line that is technically accurate and believable. Heinlein was also a pioneer in science-fiction filmmaking.

Suggested Reading

Isaac Asimov, *Nightfall and Other Stories* (New York: Doubleday, 1969).

Ray Bradbury, *Twice Twenty-Two* (New York: Doubleday, 1966).

————, *The Machineries of Joy* (New York: Simon & Schuster, 1964).

Robert Heinlein, "The Roads Must Roll," from Robert Silverberg, ed., *Science Fiction Hall of Fame* (Vol. 1) (New York: Doubleday, 1970).

———, "Universe," from Ben Bova, ed., *Science Fiction Hall of Fame* (Vol. 2) (New York: Doubleday, 1973).

C. S. Lewis, *Perelandra* (New York: Macmillan, 1944).

George Orwell, *1984* (New York: Harcourt Brace Jovanovich, 1949).

J. R. R. Tolkien, *Lord of the Rings* (New York: Houghton Mifflin, 1965). Reprinted in paperback by Ballantine Books, 1973.

7

The Dramatic Forms

The dramatic forms, which employ both sights and sounds and in addition depend upon intermediaries (actors and directors) to interpret them, are the most difficult of the writing arts. They are also the most restrictive as far as structure is concerned. Despite experiments dramatists have made in varying uses of time, successful playwrights, including those in the Theater of the Absurd, use forward-moving periods of time and conform largely to the crisis-to-climax structure. (An exception is Arthur Miller's use of the flashback in *Death of a Salesman* and *After the Fall*.) In basic structure, there is little difference between Robert Bolt's *A Man for All Seasons* and the classical dramas. The modern film, though less restricted than the staged play, tends to be forward-moving in time and tight in structure, partly because of the film industry's dependence upon stage productions for its most successful films. The telefilm, cut to a precise pattern, is the most severely structured of all the dramatic forms.

THE PLAY

The length itself, or the playing time of the drama, is a significant factor. In a more leisurely time audiences were willing to spend five hours watching a Eugene O'Neill drama. However, only an extraordinary dramatic event will hold a modern theater for

47

much more than two hours. The playwright today must therefore think in terms of a full-length drama playing a little over two hours or of two or three one-act plays that can be presented in that length of time.

The playwright has first to determine whether his dramatic idea has the scope of an evening-long play or whether he should limit it to one act. The long play corresponds in story scope and total effect to the novel, and the one-act play corresponds to a short story. The protagonist of the full-length play is involved in a conflict with life or his world, and the end effect is a comprehensive unified one. The conflict in the one-act play is a more personal, more individual one, and the end effect is a single compelling one. The protagonist of Arthur Miller's *A View from the Bridge* battles his entire world for his own survival and recognition. The protagonist of Edward Albee's one-act *The Zoo Story* seeks, in single combat with his adversary, to find his identity; only he himself is involved.

The Full-Length Play

Once he knows that his subject matter is adequate for a full-length play, the playwright blocks out his material into its major divisions (acts) and determines what each act shall contain. There is no prescribed number of acts, but there is a trend today toward the tight two-act drama with a single expressionistic stage set. The number of acts, of course, depends on the play content. Albee's *Who's Afraid of Virginia Woolf?* falls into three acts, a division so important that the playwright gives titles to the acts: "Fun and Games," "Walpurgisnacht," and "The Exorcism." *A View from the Bridge* divides naturally into two acts. It is a story of crime and punishment, crime in the first act, punishment in the second. Albee's play has a single realistic set, Miller's a single expressionistic one.

The writer has much to accomplish in his first act if he is going to get his audience back for the second one.

DRAMATIC QUESTION.   First he establishes his dramatic question. This is the question that seizes his audience. It is the lowest level of the play, but without it there is no drama. The dramatic question of *Virginia Woolf*, obvious in the first minutes of the play, is: In the battles of the sexes, who is going to be the winner? The audience of *The Zoo Story* asks immediately: What in the world is wrong with this fellow? Long before the theme is apparent in *A View from the Bridge*, the audience is asking whether Eddie Carbone can get away with his incestuous love for his niece. The dramatic question carries the suspense all the way to the final curtain, and commits the audience if it is going to be committed.

STRUCTURE. In time the first act will introduce all the characters, the theme or thesis, the overall conflict, and the immediate conflict, and it will end with the curtain descending upon a seemingly unsolvable conflict between two well-matched adversaries. The second or the second and third acts will rise in intensity from crisis to crisis to the inevitable climax and the resolution. Every element in both or all acts will contribute to the powerful unified effect at the end.

Having determined the major happenings of his two or three acts, the writer then blocks out the scenes that will compose his play, not the arbitrary Scene 1, Scene 2 on the program but the constant and invisible scene-changing that takes place every time a character enters or leaves the stage.

By approaching his play visually (people go to hear a concert but to see and hear a play), the playwright avoids the dangers of too much exposition, too many long speeches, and a static quality that may result from the lack of action and inadequate or meaningless stage business.

A part of the visual play is the action. Action includes the plot, the stage business, and the entrances and exits. None of these elements can exist for its own sake; all must contribute to the theme, the characterizations, the total effect.

DIALOGUE. All the time the playwright is looking at his play, he is listening to it, asking himself how it is going to sound to other people when it is being spoken by still other people.

The playwright knows that dialogue is the substance of his play. Dialogue is the spoken word that sounds like conversation; it must seem natural to the characters, and the theatergoer should have the feeling that he has heard people talk like that. However, there is an enormous difference between conversation and usable dialogue. Most actual conversations are meager, awkward, unfinished, full of superfluities, repetitious, and often pointless, but the dialogue of a play must be meaningful and purposeful. Each word of dialogue must advance the play in some way.

Dialogue is important in the revelation and development of the characters. The first few lines of A *View from the Bridge* point to the major flaw in Eddie Carbone's character.

Dialogue advances the story line. The quite natural dialogue among Eddie, Catherine, and Beatrice in the play's first scene tells us that Beatrice's two Italian cousins have been able to enter the country illegally and will be protected by the Carbones.

Dialogue gives the spectator a great deal of factual information that isn't sufficiently dramatic to be played on the stage. For example, Catherine, Eddie's niece, is planning to leave school and take a job. Eddie becomes angry. He does not want her to go out into the world, beyond his protection. The entire school and job subject, with all its implications and its effect on the characters, is presented in tight, significant, natural dialogue.

The tone and atmosphere of a play are determined by the dialogue as well as the stage sets. The theme or thesis is revealed by dialogue and action. Dialogue also sets and changes the pace of a play.

A novelist may allow a character to meander a little in the conversational field, to pontificate and to make speeches. The playwright, however, has to be much more selective and must keep his dialogue compressed and to the point. This sense of dialogue is important to the playwright, and even before he starts the play he should master it.

The One-Act Play

The form of the one-act play is highly controlled, with the climax coming soon after the beginning of the play. In *The Zoo Story*, the story begins just forty minutes before the accidental killing of Jerry by Peter, who is Jerry's adversary. Peter is appalled by the killing, and so is the audience. But the audience accepts it as inevitable and believable. In the one-act play the crises are reached swiftly and contribute directly and immediately to the climax.

In *The Zoo Story* the burden of the play is carried almost altogether by the dialogue. The single effect of Ionesco's *The Chairs*, on the other hand, is achieved mainly by the writer's use of doors, chairs, and stage business. Although restrained by form, the writer of the one act play is free in his choice of subject matter, characters, and dramatic approach. It is interesting to observe that whatever the subject or the form, every play presents a dramatic question.

THE MOTION-PICTURE FILM

The motion-picture writer has two choices: He may present his drama in the form of a story treatment of about fifty to sixty pages, or he may write the complete filmscript of about 120 pages.

The story treatment is written in the present tense and is a detailed summary of the plot. It contains no long involved explanations and no complicated characterizations. It merely states that this happened and then something else happened. It is accompanied by a list of the characters and a brief description of them. When it reaches the studio, a one-page summary will be made of this long story treatment for distribution to the various departments. The essential characteristic of the story treatment is clarity, which is achieved by the selection of significant details.

An awareness of trends in the motion-picture industry may determine the success of the scriptwriter. With the development of television, the film industry sought to combat it with gigantic films and with films whose subject matter would be taboo in the average living room. This trend continues, but another is now apparent: The ninety-minute movie (plus commercials) on television is enticing viewers away from the regular television shows, and some of the studios are beginning to accumulate a backlog of new movies in anticipation of this inexhaustible market.

The scriptwriter, unlike the novelist, functions in a large community of workers. He may turn his script over to it, or he may work with the group: producer, director, assistant directors, actors, cameramen, electricians, wardrobe workers, research people, editors, script revisers, script girls, technical advisers, musicians, and the many other people needed to make a film out of his script.

The important organs of a good scriptwriter are his eyes and ears. When the writer has assured himself that his story has the scope of a ninety-minute or two-hour movie (the scope of a novel or a three-act play), he puts his eyes and ears to work.

The talents of the novelist and the scriptwriter are not necessarily interchangeable. Frequently they are at war. The scriptwriter has mainly to see scenes and hear dialogue. Where the novelist may reveal or develop his characters at length, the scriptwriter can do little except describe them briefly in his script and hope that the actors will come fairly close to what he has in mind. The effects of tone, mood, and atmosphere inherent in the novelist's writing will be achieved not by the scriptwriter but by the director and his staff of technicians.

The scriptwriter's talents are closer to those of the playwright, but they are not altogether the same. The playwright has to see his play in blocks of scenes, but he does not have to see them in continuous flow. He is limited to the physical stage, but the scriptwriter has no physical limitations at all. This somewhat static quality of the live play is the reason for its weakness when a producer tries to film it exactly as it is presented on the stage.

Structure

The beginning film writer should prepare for himself a complete treatment of his story in narrative form. The more detailed it is, the easier it will be for him to come back and see and hear the scenes and dialogue he is going to write.

The second step is a blocking-out of the major scenes. Like the novel, the play, and the short story, the film rises to crisis, to another crisis, and finally to a climax and a resolution, for this is the way people want a story to be told.

Like other fiction, the film has a theme, specific conflicts, problems to be solved, and a point of view. The point of view is the writer with a camera. As in other fiction, the problem or problems belong to the protagonist who will solve (or refuse to solve) them. He will have an antagonist or antagonists, people or forces of nature. The film has a theme because it has to be about something. It does not necessarily have a thesis unless it is a so-called thesis play. (Ibsen's *Ghosts* is a thesis play, or a play with a social conscience.)

Then, creatively conscious of the equipment at his disposal, cameras and lights, the film writer carefully writes out his scenes. He is also aware that what is to be seen and heard must be seen and heard in from 90 to 110 minutes, the length of time allowed for the standard feature film. If his story scope is right, this will be no problem. When he finishes, he will have about 120 pages of typescript.

As he writes his script, he realizes that he is going to write only what shows on the screen. While this objective treatment is restrictive in one sense, it is liberating in another. He is free from exposition and description. Unlike Melville, he does not have to describe the white whale; he only has to ask for one to appear: (LONG SHOT: White whale).

What the film writer does concern himself with is action and stage business. It is not only what the character says that reveals him but what he does. The film has no time for prolonged chatter nor for the devices used by novelists to develop character. The characters must be presented on the run; a small bit of action must reveal their penury, their courage, their despair, their poverty, their egotism, their selflessness.

A feeling for pace and for timing will dictate the film's flow of scenes. The professional writer knows exactly how long he should sustain a scene of anguish, terror, anger, or even silliness. He knows at what moment he must give the viewer some relief, a change of pace and mood.

Dialogue

The writer's sharp ear for dialogue is as important as his eye for scene. As in a play, every word of dialogue must count for something: to advance the plot, to reveal the theme, to reveal the character. And while it is counting for something, it has to seem natural. It has to seem like conversation.

Effect

The total—action, sets, dialogue—must bring about the desired unified effect the writer has worked for. All of this must be visible and playable before the directors and technicians take over the script.

The film writer will present his script according to a standard form which is easily attainable in most public libraries. He limits himself to long shots, medium shots, close shots, and panoramic shots and to the designation of exteriors and interiors. He does not concern himself with camera angles and ways of achieving various lighting effects. He merely indicates what effects he wants.

The Market

It is essential for the writer to offer his work through a Hollywood or a New York agent. It is categorically impossible for an unknown free-lance writer to get his script even as far as the reception desk of a studio without the help of an agent.

THE TELEPLAY

The dramatic writer has three opportunities in television: to write an hour or a half-hour play, to create a new series, and to write a play for an established and continuous series. Whatever he chooses to do, he must constantly be aware of this: Once he has his subject matter, form is absolute. He may have the greatest play since *Hamlet* and the highest paid actors in Hollywood, but the form is invariable.

Whether he has a ninety-minute drama or an hour or a half-hour play depends upon the scope of his material as in the other writing arts. A ninety-minute teleplay is roughly equivalent to a full-length live drama or to a compact novel. A sixty-minute play has the scope of a novelette with its strong single effect. The thirty-minute teleplay is equivalent to a very short story or a one-act play which can be subdivided. The intelligent writer will give time and thinking to his scope. He will avoid thinning out a short-story idea to cover an hour play, just as he will avoid jamming into a half hour a story situation that needs at least an hour.

The teleplaywright must first conform to the actual playing time on television. For the hour play he will prepare a script for approximately forty-five minutes. The playing time of the half-hour show is about twenty-two minutes.

Next, the writer must adapt his script to the commercials which have become fixed as to length of time and placement.

The typical hour-long script of about sixty typewritten pages is divided into five parts or as follows: the tease and the first commercial, act one and the quarter-past commercial, act two and the half-past commercial, act three and the quarter-of commercial, act four and the final commercial.

This script's playing time is approximately as follows: the tease, one minute; act one, fourteen minutes; act two, twelve minutes; act three, eleven minutes; act four, seven minutes. Time adjustments are made, of course, but in general are not more than a minute or two one way or the other. Each page of the telescript allows about 1.1 minutes of playing time.

Dramatically, the writer has a four-act play. The tease is sometimes lifted out of the middle of the play at some climactic moment and presented before the opening commercial. The tease is now well established in television, for it has proved effective in keeping the viewer from changing to another channel. Sometimes the tease is the very beginning of the play, if the beginning is strong enough to keep the viewer in his chair. It rarely lasts more than sixty seconds, and for the play it is a matter of life or death. Whereas the theatergoer may not like the play he is seeing, he isn't going to walk out and buy a ticket at another theater. It is easy enough to change channels on a television set.

Structure

The teleplay itself follows the form of any tightly written drama. It presents the dramatic question, an immediate problem, a theme or thesis, the overall conflict, the crisis needed to reach a climax, and a resolution.

Because the teleplaywright has less freedom in the matter of length and time than the writer for live theater, he must even more carefully block out his scenes and rigorously control the pace. He must include only what is vital to the story, and he must think visually every minute. The teleplay is to be seen and heard, but mainly to be seen. Exposition, weak in any fictional art form, is death on television. Characterization has to be revealed quickly, believably, and visually. The plot has to move steadily on the screen before the eyes of the viewer.

When the writer blocks out his first act, he makes certain that before the next commercial he has introduced all his characters and given his protagonist a dominant trait and a problem to solve. He has given his protagonist an adversary who may or may not be the love interest. He has made the theme or thesis apparent and has presented the initial or immediate problem. And he has reached a crisis in the dramatic structure that will bring the viewer back after the commercial. This crisis is equivalent to the first curtain in live theater.

During the twelve minutes of act two, the protagonist moves toward his major crisis, his biggest obstacle.

Act three, a little shorter than the preceding acts, builds to the climax of the play, the highest point of the drama.

Act four, the briefest act, is the resolution, physical and psychological. In terms of the film, this is the chase or the pursuit, although not necessarily a physical one.

Whether the teleplay is a drama, a comedy, or a melodrama, the form is the same throughout the four acts. The four-act form is also the same for the hour-long play written for a specific running series or for a plot film introducing a new series.

Despite the restrictions on form and on subject matter, the teleplaywright has some advantages over the theater playwright. His play is going to be filmed. He will therefore not be limited to one or two stage sets. He can send his characters all over New York, Paris, or Vienna, across oceans, up and down mountains or the Empire State Building, at the same time preserving his unity of action. He can show the passing of time in ways that are impossible on the stage. He has a more liberal use of makeup, sound effects, music, and lighting. Every technical aid in the film industry is available to him.

The Market

Like the filmscript, the telescript is prepared according to a standard form.

The writer who believes he has a marketable idea for a new television series may present it in a story treatment form, or he may write the pilot film and outline a few additional episodes.

The pilot film needs careful planning. It has to introduce the members of the regular cast, indicating what their dominant traits will be; it must indicate the purpose or theme of the show and its distinguishing characteristic. If the pilot can suggest or imply some kind of unity for the whole series, the writer has a double chance of marketing it.

If the writer has an extraordinary story idea for a series, he may give it a detailed story treatment and outline briefly a few episodes. Story treatments are generally written in the present tense and include sharp characterizations of the cast. A five-page summary of the story is adequate for an hour show.

The writer may also present an episode idea for a running series in the story treatment manner, or he may prefer to write the teleplay himself.

When he writes an episode for an established series, the writer must do exactly that. It is not enough to write a dramatic teleplay and hopefully suggest that it be adapted to the series. The writer should be familiar with the series, know the members of the regular cast and their particular virtues and weaknesses, be completely aware of the plot pattern and subject matter. He must follow the unchanging pattern and make use of the established cast.

The teleplaywright must remember that he writes not for a large audience seated in a theater but for one or two (perhaps as many as five) people in a living room. The stage, so to speak, is no more than six or seven feet from the viewer's face. The writer does not have a specific audience of dedicated theatergoers. He is more likely to have as an audience a family of assorted ages. He lacks the aesthetic distance of the live theater and the motion-picture theater. What is bearable at a distance of a hundred feet is not bearable across the living room.

Over a period of time, television writers have learned to distinguish between the bearable and the unbearable. Killings are endlessly tolerated if they are quick and not too realistic; prolonged lovemaking, quite acceptable in motion pictures, is taboo in the living room. Obscene language, acceptable in all the other visual arts, is objectionable five feet away. The breaking of all Ten Commandments, as in *Peyton Place*, is bearable, but generally sexual perversions are not. Sometimes it is not the subject matter but the way it is handled that makes it bearable or unbearable for the living-room spectator. If the adulterer is clean, well-dressed, and sorrowful, he may stay in the living room. The soiled drug addict must be hurried off.

Remember: Dialogue is the substance of the play.

Start Writing!

1. Write a page of dialogue that might be taking place between a person you like and someone you do not like.
2. If you could talk to anyone who has ever lived, whom would you choose? Write two pages of dialogue between you and that person.
3. Write a page of dialogue between a male chauvinist and a radical feminist.
4. Write one page of dialogue between two six-year-old children, one gregarious and one introverted, who meet during recess on their first day at school.

5. Testing Your Dialogue
   Write a passage of dialogue that occurs in the opening situation of your story. Then ask yourself:
   a. Does it reveal the identity of your speakers?
   b. Is the idiom natural to the person who is speaking?
   c. Blending with narration and description, does it establish
   the setting?
   d. Does it project the relationship between the people involved?
   e. Does it point toward a new situation in which these same
   characters will find themselves as the story progresses?
   f. Is it free of trite phrases, aimless or repetitious sentences?
6. Analyze Joyce Carol Oates's short story "Upon the Sweeping
   Flood" as a sixty-minute TV drama, making the points of crisis
   explicit.
7. Select a novel and rewrite it into dramatic form as a full-length
   play.
8. Write a ninety-minute satirical television comedy, western,
   mystery, or adventure.

Suggested Reading

Edward Albee, *All Over* (New York: Atheneum, 1971).

———, *Who's Afraid of Virginia Woolf?* (New York: Atheneum,
1962).

———, *The Zoo Story* (New York: Coward, McCann, and Geog-
hegan, 1960).

Ed Bullins, "The Electronic Nigger," from *Five Plays* (New York:
Bobbs-Merrill, 1969).

Rolf Hocchuth, *Soldiers* (New York: Grove, 1968).

Langston Hughes, "Mother and Child," from King and Milner,
eds., *Black Drama Anthology* (New York: Columbia University
Press, 1972).

Arthur Miller, *A View from the Bridge* (New York: Viking,
1957).

Neil Simon, *The Sunshine Boys* (New York: Random House,
1973).

————, *Last of the Red Hot Lovers* (New York: Random House, 1970).
Tennessee Williams, *The Milk Train Doesn't Stop Here Anymore* (New York: New Directions, 1973).

8

The People in Fiction

A well-written story is usually about a human being who, for the period of time the story lasts, is worth writing about. He is real, he is interesting, and he engages the reader.

In his search for real and interesting characters, the beginning writer must beware of two weaknesses: copying a character directly from life instead of selecting the characteristics that make the man seem real and believable and using stock or stereotyped characters.

Katherine Anne Porter said that she wrote entirely from memory and that she derived the characters in her stories from people she had known or had heard about. However, when her character finally emerged, he may have been a composite of several people she remembered. She selected qualities and traits of one man and added to them the characteristics or physical attributes of another to introduce a real and believable person.

Using stereotyped characters is the timid writer's approach. The mousy librarian, the absentminded professor, and the prostitute with the heart of gold have been written about so often that they seem real and therefore safe to the beginning writer. The easiest way to avoid stock characters is simply to stop thinking about people as stereotypes. I have watched beginning writers develop excellent stories merely by trying to write a paragraph about a schoolteacher who was not a stock figure or about a teenager who was not a typical teenager.

ATTRIBUTES

The character in a story has three things: a physical body, an inner consciousness, and a time and place. As a human being he has them in total. In total, however, he is no more than a case history for a sociologist, a psychologist, or a historian. And this is where the artistry of the writer makes its entrance. This is the pleasure and the fun of the writer: to select from these three elements and to create from the person's chaotic world some meaningful unity. From the person's physical attributes, inner life, and external life he must select those characteristics that contribute to a story and illuminate a theme.

In a short story it is hardly possible to present all the characters as completely known people. The writer will develop his protagonist as three-dimensionally as possible, but he will be forced to limit the development of his minor characters. However briefly any character may be developed, he does not have to be a stereotype. The grandmother of Flannery O'Connor's "A Good Man Is Hard to Find" is revealed three-dimensionally, and the reader feels that he has actually met this woman whose dominant trait is her inexhaustible capacity for self-indulgence. The other characters are believable, too, even though the reader knows less about them, but what is known about them contributes to the development of the story. The distinguishing characteristic of the killer is his profound concern with the life and death of Jesus Christ. This is not the customary image of a killer, but in this story it seems real and believable.

External Attributes

It is essential for a writer to write down a great deal more about his people than he will be able to use. Even though he will use little or no physical or outside descriptions of his characters, he should put down on a piece of paper all their physical attributes. He may use none of them except a man's hands, for example, but he will see the hands in relation to the rest of the man. If the hands have meaning for the writer, they will have it for the reader. Just the way the grandmother wears her hat on the long car trip or even the fact that she wears a hat at all is illuminating to the story. The important physical attribute of Miss Emily in Faulkner's "A Rose for Emily" is the color of her hair. It is significant through the last line of the story.

Internal Attributes

The person of a story also has invisible attributes inside his body. He has memories, ideas, feelings, emotions, virtues. The writer must know all about the interior of his people, no matter how little he uses in his final revelation.

We can imagine Flannery O'Connor thinking about the grandmother, a seemingly nice little old woman and a proper Christian. What else? On the first page she is seen to be a stubborn woman, determined to go on the family's trip even though the children would be happier without her. Then what? Self-centered and bossy, she imposes her own desires on the family, prevails upon them to go where she wants to go. Later her vanity keeps her from acknowledging that she has brought them on a senseless detour. Her willfulness—she has carried along her cat which causes the car accident—leads them to the three killers. Her complete devotion to her own skin keeps her begging for her life while her son, her daughter-in-law, and her two grandchildren are being murdered. We can imagine O'Connor's notes on the protagonist of her story: a churchgoing old lady, stubborn, bossy, self-centered, vain, willful, monstrously egotistical. We can imagine her saying: What kind of situation would most compellingly reveal these traits? Or she might have reversed the procedure and asked: What traits could be revealed by a woman in this particular situation?

Consistency is important in careful characterization. A character may change, of course, but the change must be motivated.

Throughout "A Rose for Emily" Miss Emily is consistently a female member of a decadent, aristocratic Southern family. Even her murder of her lover seems consistent and therefore believable.

Environment

In addition to his external and internal attributes, the person in a story has an environment. Much of where he is going depends upon his time and his place. The small Southern town environment of the grandmother is partly responsible for what happened to the family in "A Good Man Is Hard to Find," just as the killer's environment also leads to his particular crime. The awful African sun is partly responsible for the slaying in Camus' *The Stranger*. A riot takes place in a city in August that would not have taken place in December.

METHODS OF CHARACTERIZATION

Characters in a story are disclosed to the reader in two general ways: by development and revelation. The writer may develop (show the change in) his character before the eyes of the reader, or he may slowly reveal a totally conceived character. Faulkner developed Miss Emily, showing her reactions to the events in her life. O'Connor revealed or uncovered the grandmother little by little. *The Stranger* was developed. The minister in Tennessee Williams's *Night of the Iguana* was developed. Willy Loman in *Death of a Salesman* was uncovered.

Exposition

The least compelling and the least economical way of presenting a character is by pure exposition, a method loved in the leisurely nineteenth century. Today's writer rarely explains his character; he allows the character's words, reactions, and deeds to explain him. The people in Hemingway's "The Killers," for example, reveal themselves almost altogether by what they say.

Dialogue

A story is largely about people talking to one another. Even in stories of physical action and violence, only a small percentage of time is spent running, shooting, beating, looting, ravishing, fighting, killing. Most of the time people are talking, just as in real life.

Actually, dialogue is action, too, for conversation is something happening; it is something two people do with each other. It is not a static situation and should never be used as such by the writer. Idle chitchat should not be used in a story unless it reveals character.

Because it has to appear real without being real, dialogue requires more art than any other factor in fiction. It has to seem spontaneous, fragmented, irrelevant, halting; yet at the same time it must be intentional and meaningful. Every sentence must be descriptive of the person speaking.

The writer must be forever listening, his ears sensitive to the rhythm and intonation of ordinary speech. And when he writes his dialogue, he should read it aloud to hear how it sounds.

Dialogue between two people may introduce and interpret the character and personality of a third person, at the same time revealing something of their own characters.

In her *New Yorker* story, "The Jockey," Carson McCullers introduced her three characters through a conversation between the two minor characters, Sylvester and a bookie named Simmons. The fairly brief opening dialogue reveals the dominant traits of the two men and presents the entire background of the jockey, the protagonist of the story. The ensuing dialogue among the three men tells the whole story.

Inner Monologue

Inner (or interior) monologue is a convenient and effective method of introducing and developing characterization. Mr. Martin through inner monologue introduces the character of Mrs. Barrows in the James Thurber story, "The Catbird Seat."

The woman had appalled Mr. Martin instantly, but he hadn't shown it. He had given her his dry hand, a look of studious concentration, and a faint smile. "Well," she had said, looking at the papers on his desk, "are you lifting the oxcart out of the ditch?" As Mr. Martin recalled that moment, over his milk, he squirmed slightly. He must keep his mind on her crimes as a special adviser, not on her peccadillos as a personality.

Thurber used the inner monologue device to tell the entire story.

Narration

Another way of projecting character or personality is by simple narration, showing what a person did and how he did it: the way a man drives on a freeway; the way he eats his breakfast; the way he walks his wife's dog; his behavior when he is drunk, in a poker game, with his children, in an accident, while his wife is having a baby. The writer can learn much by watching how people do things, particularly when they are under stress, and writing down in detail what they do, how they look, and what they say.

The character of a story may be indicated, too, by what he wears, what he owns, what he values, and what he does not value. A description of what a woman wears to go shopping in a supermarket may be more revealing than pages of exposition by the writer.

Start Writing!

1. The painter's approach to characterization (Flaubert's) is considered old-fashioned by today's writers who prefer to present a character through monologue or dialogue, or to show him through external objects, ordinary activities, and so on. Introduce a character who interests you in the following ways:
   a. through his own inner monologue
   b. through two people discussing him in his absence
   c. through a dialogue between himself and another person
   d. show him driving a car or shaving
   e. describe the possessions he values
   f. describe his hands and the way he uses them.

Suggested Reading

John Barth, *Chimera* (long short stories) (New York: Random House, 1972).

Maeve Brennan, *Christmas Eve* (short stories) (New York: Scribner's, 1974).

John Cheever, *World of Apples* (New York: Knopf, 1973).

Mavis Gallant, *The Pegnitz Junction: A Novella and Five Short Stories*. New York, Random House, 1973.

Ernest Hemingway, *Short Stories of Ernest Hemingway* (New York: Scribner's, 1955).

Joyce Carol Oates, *Marriages and Infidelities* (New York: Vanguard, 1972).

Flannery O'Connor, *A Good Man Is Hard to Find* (New York: Harcourt Brace Jovanovich, 1955).

John O'Hara, *The Time Element and Other Stories* (New York: Random House, 1972).

Katherine Anne Porter, *Collected Stories of Katherine Anne Porter* (New York: Harcourt Brace Jovanovich, 1965).

John Updike, *Museums & Women & Other Stories* (New York: Knopf, 1972).

9

Structure and Pattern

When a building has been completed or a song has been sung, the viewer or the listener is unaware of its structure. Yet the framework is there. The artist put it there. In the same way, the reader should be unaware of the structure (form or pattern) of an excellent piece of writing. The structure should be visible only to the writer.

There is virtually no limit to the structural patterns used by writers of nonformula or quality stories. The pattern may be a simple straight line like that of Katherine Mansfield's "Bliss"; it may be a complicated pattern like that of Faulkner's "A Rose for Emily."

"Bliss," following a straight, slightly rising line, consists of a series of incidents showing that a woman's feeling of bliss is based on her immaturity, and through the use of symbols, foreshadowing her disillusion. The straight structural line carries the story to the end of the day and to the shocking end of her state of bliss.

"A Rose for Emily" is a structural masterpiece. The time span is sixty years. The story begins and ends in the present, but the writer uses a half-dozen time periods, all out of sequence. Yet the story moves continuously and freely to the horrifying climax and the single devastating effect, with the reader unaware of the structural complexities.

The simplest pattern is the one that is characteristic of what we call the *New Yorker* story (no matter what magazine publishes it). This pattern is a straight line moving horizontally all the way to the end. The single effect which all short stories must have is achieved by the amassing of details that push the story forward.

The total structure of a piece of fiction is determined largely by the point of view, the conflict and crises, and the writer's use of time spans.

TYPES OF STORY STRUCTURE

If an animal body had no bone structure, it would be nothing but a blob and flesh and blood, going nowhere, doing nothing. So it is with a short story or actually with any piece of writing. A story is something that goes somewhere on its feet and does something with its hands. It doesn't just sit there like a carrot contemplating its vitamins. A completely structured or plotted story, complete with crises and climax, looks like this:

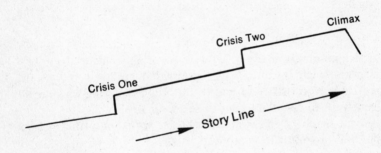

Introduction of:

    characters
    problem
    theme
    tone
    setting
    point of view

The story with little plot complication that rises slightly toward a climax looks like this:

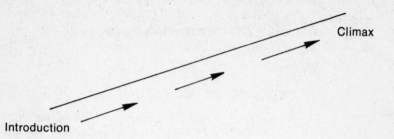

The flat (*New Yorker*) type of story, depending on an accumulation of interesting relevant details, looks like this:

Introduction   details   details   details   details   details   Ending

It is important for the writer to know exactly where his story is going and what it will do when it arrives. You have heard people say that they just sit down and write without knowing where their characters will take them. But these are amateurs. They are people who just sit down and write. In all three structural plans, motion (physical or spiritual) is involved.

POINT OF VIEW

The point of view is where the writer is sitting. It is not to be confused with focus, which is where he keeps his eyes.

Whatever point of view is used, it affects all other aspects of the story: the characterization, the plot development, the tone, the style, and of course, the focus. The point of view is no whimsical thing. The writer must select it carefully, for it must be organic to the story. It must be inevitable.

Author Omniscient

The writer may choose to write from a heavenly cloud, in which case he uses the point of view of the author omniscient. He can shift his focus from one character to another; he may present his characters in a three-dimensional or two-dimensional manner; he can enter anybody's mind; he may instruct, explain, interpret, be as objective or as subjective as he pleases.

An example of the full-blown, all-out author-omniscient point of view is Melville's *Moby Dick*. Saul Bellow's novel *Herzog* illustrates a more restrained use of this point of view. Twentieth-century novelists may write from the clouds, but unlike nineteenth-century writers, they rarely editorialize, preach, or project their own personalities into their works. Short-story writers seldom use the author-omniscient point of view. It is difficult to give a story the tightness and unity it needs without using a more limited point of view. Thomas Mann's "Disorder and Early Sorrow" and D. H. Lawrence's "The Rocking Horse Winner" are successfully told from the omniscient point of view, but they are quite long stories, skillfully handled. Writers today usually limit their use of the omniscient point of view to works in which the span of time and space is large and the story scope is extensive.

First Person

The writer may choose to tell his story in the first person. As the narrator, he may be involved as the protagonist or as a minor character. Or he may not be involved at all; he is then merely a spectator or a "people-watcher." Under no circumstances may he look into the minds of other characters. He may only speculate.

Novelists rarely use the first-person narration since it is difficult to sustain interest through this single point of view. Writers of short suspense novels sometimes find it effective. This point of view was advantageous to the writer of *Robinson Crusoe*; it would be ridiculous and boring in a novel like *War and Peace* or *Gone With the Wind*.

The first person has certain advantages: First, it gives a certain illusion of reality; second, it certainly gives an easy structure to a story, for the narrator can go back and forth in time without contriving transitions.

On the other hand, it demands specific technical skills. The author must place himself in the mind of the narrator and stay there. In a story like Ring Lardner's "Haircut" the author must remain within the vocabulary and the limited insight and intelligence of a small-town barber. The first-person narrator is also necessarily restrained as far as he himself as a character is concerned. His own qualities of heroism and nobility or sensitivity, for example, have to be treated with care or they will emerge without conviction.

Writers of the reminiscent kind of story prefer the first-person narrator point of view. In the following excellent and economical first paragraph of "My Oedipus Complex," Frank O'Connor established point of view, time, and tone. He also introduced his two major characters.

> Father was in the army through the war . . . so up to the age of five, I never saw much of him, and what I saw did not worry me. Sometimes I woke and there was a big figure in khaki peering down at me in the candlelight. Sometimes in the early morning I heard the slamming of the front door and the clatter of nailed boots down the cobbles of the lane. These were Father's entrances and exits. Like Santa Claus he came and went mysteriously.*

Arthur Koestler used the same point of view though the tone is altogether different in "Portrait of the Author at Sixteen." This is his first paragraph:

> I emerged from childhood an exasperating and pathetic figure. Almost the whole of my adolescence is painful to remember. For a period of two or three years, Cyril Connolly's remark about his youth was equally true of mine: I have always disliked myself at any given moment: the sum of these moments is my life.

Whatever the tone, amusing like Eudora Welty's "Why I Live at the P.O.," dramatic like John Cheever's "The Angel of the

* Frank O'Connor, "My Oedipus Complex," from *Stories* (New York: Vintage, 1956).

Bridge," or suspenseful as in Edgar Allan Poe's "The Fall of the House of Usher," the use of the first person gives an immediacy that another point of view might fail to give.

Third Person

Within the framework of the third person, the writer has, in addition to the author-omniscient approach, three alternatives: the third-person limited point of view, the third-person subjective point of view, and the third-person objective point of view.

THIRD-PERSON LIMITED. The third-person limited point of view keeps the entire story inside the world of one character, revealing to the reader only what this character knows and experiences. The difference between this and the first-person narrator is merely in the use of the pronoun "he" or "she" instead of "I." Third-person limited achieves a tightness and a unity characteristic of most stories being written today.

Ernest Hemingway began his story "Ten Indians" by establishing this limited point of view: "After one Fourth of July, Nick, driving home late from town in the big wagon with Joe Garner and his family, passed nine drunken Indians along the road." The story of Nick's love for the tenth Indian and his eventual disillusion when his father tells him about her promiscuity is told altogether through what Nick hears from other people and through his own reaction to what he hears. Hemingway stepped briefly into Nick's mind in the last paragraph as Nick remembers, then forgets his love. "In the morning there was a big wind blowing and the waves were running high up on the beach and he was awake a long time before he remembered that his heart was broken."

William Saroyan wrote "The Daring Young Man on the Flying Trapeze" from this point of view. Another example is "The New Dress" by Virginia Woolf.

THIRD-PERSON SUBJECTIVE. Less limited is the third-person subjective point of view, which enables the protagonist to interpret and explain the actions and experiences of other characters. The writer remains altogether in the mind of the protagonist but allows the protagonist to speculate.

In the first paragraph of Katherine Anne Porter's "The Jilting of Granny Weatherall," we recognize the third-person subjective point of view.

> She flicked her wrist neatly out of Doctor Harvy's pudgy careful fingers and pulled the sheet up to her chin. The brat ought to be in knee breeches. Doctoring around the country with spectacles on his nose! "Get along now, take your schoolbooks and go. There's nothing wrong with me."

Granny Weatherall is dying, and inside her mind, which goes back and forth from the present to sixty years before, Mrs. Porter told the story of a woman who had waited with her priest for a bridegroom who never came, a woman who had weathered the tragedy and had lived a seemingly rich and splendid life. Through Granny's mind, Mrs. Porter presented the many characters who shared the protagonist's life. As Granny dies, without the presence of her favorite child Hapsy, she reflects upon her second tragic disappointment:

> For the second time there was no sign. Again no bridegroom and the priest in the house. She could not remember any other sorrow because this grief wiped them all away. . . . She stretched herself with a deep breath and blew out the light.

Other stories related from this point of view are Katherine Mansfield's "Bliss," John Steinbeck's "The Leader of the People," John Updike's "A Sense of Shelter," and F. Scott Fitzgerald's "Babylon Revisited."

THIRD-PERSON OBJECTIVE. Writers of the Hemingway school prefer the third-person objective point of view, which is probably the most difficult to sustain in an interesting way. The writer is a camera or a play director, and the entire story is revealed by what happens and what is said. The minds of the characters remain closed to the reader. The success of this kind of story depends upon the writer's skill in selecting the appropriate action and the revealing dialogue. Mediocre imitators of Hemingway succeed only in boring the reader.

Hemingway's "The Killers" represents this point of view perfectly. The camera and the sound track follow Nick Adams from the restaurant where he meets the killers, then up to Ole Anderson's room in the boardinghouse, and back once more to the restaurant. Only from what he allowed to happen and to be said did Hemingway tell the story of Ole Anderson's inevitable killing and Nick Adams's reactions to it. At no time did Hemingway speculate or enter the minds of his characters. Nick Adams's willingness to become involved and committed is shown by his effort to warn the victim and by his last words: "I'm going to get out of this town. . . . I can't stand to think about him waiting in the room and knowing he's going to get it. It's too damned awful."

NOVELS.   These three limited points of view are too restrictive for a long novel. To sustain interest, the novelist finds it necessary to enter the minds of all or of most of his characters and prefers the omniscient point of view. However, for the short, intense novel some modern writers use the third-person subjective point of view. An example is John Updike's *Rabbit Run*.

FOCUS

The writer never changes his point of view, but he does shift his focus. Mrs. Porter moved away from Granny Weatherall long enough to focus briefly on other characters. Hemingway shifted his focus from Nick Adams to George, to Ole Anderson, to the killers. In "Ten Indians," Hemingway moved from Nick to a half-dozen other characters in the story. However, the tighter the story, the more concentrated is the focus on the main character. It can never leave him for long. This is also true of a novel with the most relaxed omniscient point of view. The focus must shift, but the competent writer knows at what point it must return to the protagonist. In *Gone With the Wind*, Margaret Mitchell went far afield, but relentlessly she returned the focus to her two main characters, Scarlett O'Hara and Rhett Butler.

CONFLICT

The structural advancement of a piece of fiction is provided by the conflict as it is stated or implied in the beginning and rises in a series of crises to the climax and resolution. Conflict provides the suspense. It is the struggle between two opposing forces: One is a human being; the other is either another human being or a force of nature, destiny, or society. Conflict may be slight, as in Hemingway's "The Killers," or it may be a life-and-death struggle as in his *The Old Man and the Sea*. It is essential, for without it, a story is no more than a tale, an anecdote, a sketch, or an incident. The conflict may be a physical one; it may also be spiritual, emotional, or mental. A large work such as *Moby Dick* or *Julius Caesar* will probably contain more than one conflict; a tightly written short story, only one.

An important factor in conflict is equality of power, which provides the balance of the structure. The protagonist and the antagonist must be so evenly matched that both will realize, win or lose, that they have been engaged in a fight. Faust and Mephistopheles, Othello and Iago, Antigone and Creon, Ahab and the whale, the old man and the fish are all worthy adversaries. Each has a chance to win. When the writer stacks all the cards against one or the other, the resulting conflict will not hold the reader's interest. When victory or defeat is visibly predictable, the writer has probably written a bad melodrama.

THEME

Subtly accompanying the growing conflict is the theme of the story. Theme is in abstract form what the story is about and usually can be expressed in two or three words: possessive mother love, search for identity, uncontrollable ambition, and so forth. Without theme a story is nothing but a plot. A suspense story, for example, does not necessarily have a theme. The writer may be writing his story altogether for the sake of the action. A story telling how a man and woman planned and committed the murder of an old man and got caught might simply be a murder mystery. But to this action Shakespeare added the theme of uncontrollable ambition and its consequences and wrote *Macbeth*. The theme grows as the plot advances and the characters are developed or revealed.

It emerges, complete, with the climax of the story and the final revelation of the main characters.

TIME SPAN

The selection of periods of time for the duration of the story is a primary structural consideration. A story cannot be told as and when it happened. Too many irrelevant facts and details will clutter and weaken it.

Time patterns in novels vary from the simple, ever-forward direction of a Hemingway novel to the complicated montage of a James Joyce novel.

The time of William Golding's *Pincher Martin* is a few seconds, the final few seconds of a drowning man. Inside these few seconds are several periods of years, not chronologically in sequence.

The Sound and the Fury by Faulkner is made up of episodes that take place in four days; yet the time span reaches from 1910 to 1925. In this book time flows and boils up and over in the mind of a character and can leap ten years inside a single sentence.

The one day of *Ulysses* by James Joyce includes a montage of past days and periods of time superimposed upon other periods of time through the conscious and subconscious memories of the character. This is time in flow, too.

The Forward Approach

One deceptively simple use of time is Hemingway's forward approach. The writer merely selects an hour, a few hours, or perhaps a day and tells what happened chronologically during that period of time. He takes no backward look except perhaps in dialogue. The period of time for "The Killers" is no more than that required for the brief conversation with the killers, Nick's visit to their victim, and his immediate return to the restaurant.

Flannery O'Connor used time in the forward manner in "The River" and "A Good Man Is Hard to Find."

The story of "The River" begins at six o'clock in the morning when the little boy is taken to a river baptism and ends early the next morning when he drowns in that same river. From this twenty-four-hour period, O'Connor selected certain times that give the reader the illusion he has lived through the entire time, skillfully using transitions to indicate the passing of time. She revealed all that is necessary through meaningful events and dialogue. She never went back in time.

The writer used three units of time in the forward manner to tell her story, "A Good Man Is Hard to Find," about an ordinary family slain in an extraordinary manner by a homicidal maniac. The first unit consists of a few minutes the evening before the trip. The second unit is the following morning through lunchtime as the actions of the grandmother on the trip make the consequences inevitable. The third unit is a brief part of the afternoon when the misfit and his companions kill off the family in three separate shootings. The only backward look in this story is taken by the grandmother in her conversations with the other characters.

A variation on the forward use of time is illustrated by Katherine Anne Porter's "The Grave." The writer selected a short period (about an hour) from the past of the protagonist, then a period of a few minutes twenty years later. The last paragraph of "The Grave" consists of these few minutes.

Guy de Maupassant used this variation in many of his stories. He selected a significant time in the life of Madame Loisel, who borrowed a necklace from a good friend, lost it, and ruined her life and her husband's to pay for it. Then the story moves ahead many years to a chance meeting between the two women when Madame Loisel learned that the necklace she had lost was worthless.

The Flashback

The reverse of the forward use of time is the flashback, a return to the past with a new, complete time and place. This is not to be confused with simple references to the past by the writer or through dialogue.

One backward moving arrangement of time is the single flashback. William Faulkner's story "That Evening Sun" is all flash-

back except the first paragraph. The story begins in the present
tense:

> Monday is no different from any weekday in Jefferson now.
> The streets are paved now, and the telephone and electric com-
> panies are cutting down more and more shade trees . . . and
> even the Negro women who still take in white people's washing
> after the old custom, fetch and deliver it in automobiles.

Faulkner then moved smoothly into the flashback by using the
conditional tense.

> But fifteen years ago, on Monday morning, the quiet dusty streets
> would be full of Negro women with, balanced on their steady,
> turbaned heads, bundles of clothes tied up in sheets. . . .

Still in the conditional tense, Faulkner introduced Nancy, his
principal character; then two paragraphs further, he fell quite naturally into the past tense which he continued throughout the
story, never returning to the present.

A more common device is to begin in the present, flash back to
the past, then return to the present. The flashback is accompanied
by use of the past perfect tense for two or three sentences and
then a return to the simple past. To come out of the flashback
requires careful writing. Some writers merely plunge the reader
back into the scene they had abandoned for the flashback. If it is
a sufficiently contrasting scene, they can do this successfully. It is
important for the end of the flashback scene to be altogether different from the present one.

The use of multiple flashbacks requires even more skill, but can
be an effective way of unifying scattered material.

James Thurber's "The Catbird Seat" begins on a Monday night
when it shows Mr. Martin buying a pack of cigarettes in a cigar
store on Broadway. The second paragraph starts the first of a series
of flashbacks. "It was just a week to the day since Mr. Martin had
decided to rub out Mrs. Ulgine Barrows." As Martin carries
through his plan that Monday evening to rub out Mrs. Barrows,
Thurber's story returns periodically to the past (using the past
perfect tense, then the past tense) to show Martin's motivation.

The second half of the story contains no flashbacks. It is a direct account of the "rubbing out" of Mrs. Barrows.

Virginia Woolf, in "The New Dress," used the flashback masterfully. The episode itself takes place during an evening, but the writer moved ahead in time, back to the present, then to the day before, then to about thirty years before, and back to the present.

An even greater skill can be seen in Faulkner's "A Rose for Emily." The writer accomplished the near impossible: a short story whose time span is about sixty years. He started and ended with the present time, the day of the funeral, and within the story he used a half-dozen different time periods, all out of sequence. Yet the story flows freely, the reader unaware of the flashback technique.

The Once-Upon-a-Time Approach

Writers sometimes use the once-upon-a-time approach, specifying no particular periods. John Cheever's "The Angel of the Bridge" gives the reader a fairy-tale feeling of time. The opening paragraph tells about his seventy-eight-year-old mother waltzing on ice skates in Rockefeller Center, but it is once upon a time. The story is about his mother who is afraid of elevators and about himself and his fear of bridges. The times of the story are picked out of infinity, and the ending also belongs to infinity, sometime in the future. This kind of story lacks immediacy. Its success must depend upon the characterizations, the complications, and the writer's style.

Start Writing!

1. The point of view is where the writer is sitting. He may choose to write from the author-omniscient, the first-person narrative, the third-person limited, the third-person subjective, or the camera point of view. Select three of these points of view and present one character in a given situation from each of the three points of view.

2. Theme is in abstract form what the story is about and can be expressed in two or three words: possessive mother love, search for identity, and so forth. Using the theme end of innocence, discuss a possible story from your own life.
3. As far as time span is concerned you will probably prefer to use the forward approach or the flashback. The Cinderella story is always told with the forward approach. Rewrite it with the flashback approach, beginning your story with the meeting of Cinderella and the prince at the ball.

Suggested Reading

Saul Bellow, *Mosby's Memoirs* (New York: Fawcett World, 1972).

William Burroughs, *Wild Boys* (New York: Grove, 1971).

John Cheever, *The Brigadier and the Golf Widow* (New York: Harper & Row, 1964).

Joan Didion, *Play It As It Lays* (New York: Farrar, Straus & Giroux, 1970).

Shirley Ann Grau, *The Hard Blue Sky* (New York: Fawcett World, 1972).

D. H. Lawrence, *The Complete Short Stories of D. H. Lawrence* (3 vols.) (New York: Viking, 1961).

Bernard Malamud, *Rembrandt's Hat* (New York: Farrar, Straus & Giroux, 1973).

Wright Morris, *A Reader* (New York: Harper & Row, 1970).

Katherine Anne Porter, *Flowering Judas and Other Stories* (New York: New American Library, 1970).

Jesse Stuart, *32 Votes Before Breakfast* (short stories) (New York: McGraw-Hill, 1974).

10

Tone

Tone, as a literary term, has two meanings. It may be the sound of the writer's voice or the atmosphere he chooses to give to his story.

SOUND

As the sound of the writer's voice, the tone may be laughing, crying, frivolous, solemn, ironic, or any of the many other sounds made by the human voice. The voice of a story must be consistent and appropriate. The writer should not attempt to change his voice in a story any more than he should change his theme. The sound of Shirley Jackson's voice in "The Lottery" is a matter-of-fact one. It remains matter-of-fact through the last sentence. The voice should be appropriate to the subject matter and to the time in which the writer lives. A frivolous voice in a serious subject is permissible only in satire. The voice of a nineteenth-century Poe or of a sixteenth-century Shakespeare is not convincing in the twentieth century. The first paragraph of Eudora Welty's "Powerhouse" is convincing in the twentieth century.

> Powerhouse is playing! He's here on tour from the city—
> "Powerhouse and His Keyboard"—"Powerhouse and His Tas-
> manians" think of the things he calls himself. There's noone in
> the world like him. You can't tell what he is. "Niggermman"? he

looks more Asiatic, monkey, Jewish, Babylonian, Peruvian, fanatic, devil. He has pale gray eyes, heavy lids, maybe horny like a lizard's, but big glowing eyes when they're open. . . . And his mouth is going every minute. . . . Improvising, coming on a light and childish melody—smooch—he loves it with his mouth.

ATMOSPHERE

The atmosphere or tone of the story itself depends on how the writer wishes to use it. It, too, must be appropriate and consistent. A somber atmosphere dominates Edgar Allan Poe's "The Fall of the House of Usher." The story begins:

> During the whole of a dull, dark, and soundless day in the autumn of the year, when the clouds hung oppressively low in the heavens, I had been passing alone, on horseback, through a singularly dreary tract of country. . . . There was an iciness, a sinking, a sickening of the heart—an unredeemed dreariness of thought. . . .

Poe set the tone of his story in this first paragraph, then relentlessly followed it through to the last paragraph when the House of Usher was ripped apart and disappeared into "the deep and dank tarn." The somberness was achieved through Poe's selection of season, weather, words connoting his mood, and certain consonant and vowel sounds associated with oppressive images. The tone is appropriate and consistent.

Katherine Anne Porter gave to "Flowering Judas" a tone of nervous immediacy by beginning her story in the present tense and sustaining it throughout except for passages of recollection that demand a past tense.

The commonplace atmosphere of a Ring Lardner story never varies. The opening paragraph of "Golden Honeymoon" shows a typical Lardner tone:

> Mother says that when I start talking I never know when to stop. But I tell her the only time I get a chance is when she ain't around, so I have to make the most of it. I guess the fact is neither one of us would be welcome in a Quaker meeting, but as I tell Mother, what did God give us tongues for if He didn't want we should use them?

The tone remains commonplace, but the sound of the author's voice is ironic, and the single effect of the story is one of charming irony. The reader feels superior to the protagonist but becomes quite fond of him. The ordinary atmosphere is one of the factors contributing to this desirable single effect. Lardner used the same device to achieve an entirely nonhumorous single effect in "Haircut."

Shirley Jackson introduced "The Lottery" in a matter-of-fact atmosphere that helps produce a horrifying single effect. It is this commonplace tone that makes the story so terrifying. It is a midsummer day, the flowers are blooming, and the people of the village are gathering in the square for what would seem to be an innocent diversion that would allow them to get home for noon dinner. There is nothing in the atmosphere that would cause the reader to suspect that a woman was going to be stoned to death.

The commonplace tone continues with the children playing in the dust, talking about school, and picking up stones. The girls are standing around looking at the boys. The men are talking to one another about weather, taxes, and tractors. The women are gossiping among themselves. The lottery is compared with the village square dances, the teenage club, the Halloween program.

The tone continues to be casual, natural, while the drama subtly emerges. If the author had chosen a Poe-like atmosphere for "The Lottery," she would not have written such a powerful story.

The stringent, athletic prose that distinguishes Ernest Hemingway establishes the atmosphere of his story "The Battler" from its beginning:

> Nick stood up. He was all right. He looked up the track at the lights of the caboose going out of sight around the curve. There was water on both sides of the track, then tamarack swamp. He felt his knee. The pants were torn and the skin was barked. His hands were scraped and there were sand and cinders driven up under his nails. . . . He went over to the edge of the track down the little slope to the water and washed his hands. . . . He squatted down and bathed his knee. That lousy crut of a brakeman. He would get him some day.

The dreamlike, fairy-tale atmosphere of Truman Capote's "A

Diamond Guitar" is characteristic of much of his prose. It is accomplished by the writer's treatment of the various elements of the story: his characters who live on the fringes of society or "the world"; his theme that man can't bear a great deal of reality; his conflict, the prisoner's entrapment between two unreal worlds.

In the first paragraph of "Mario and the Magician," Thomas Mann explicitly set up an uneasy, disagreeable tone that persists throughout the story.

> From the first moment the air of the place made us uneasy, we felt irritable, on edge; then at the end came the shocking business of Cipolla, that dreadful being who seemed to incorporate, in so fateful and so humanly impressive a way, all the peculiar evilness of the situation as a whole.

Sometimes a writer will want the tone or atmosphere to be the prevailing element of the story, with theme, plot, character all subservient to it. An example of this is Katherine Mansfield's "Bliss." It is the tone of this story, built up by many carefully selected, sensuous details, that gives it unforgettable meaning. Without this atmosphere or tone, "Bliss" would be a somewhat meager story: A sexually unawakened woman believes herself to be blissfully happy; she is suddenly awakened to sexual desire; she finds that her husband is faithless to her and is involved with her best friend; end of bliss. The plot is not important, nor are the various meanings that might be derived from the plot: Husbands are no good; friends are not to be trusted; happiness does not endure. The writer gave the first sensual overtones to this story almost at the beginning when Bertha Young arranges the fruit bowl.

> Mary brought in the fruit on a tray and with it a glass bowl, and a blue dish, very lovely, with a strange sheen on it as though it had been dipped in milk. . . . There were tangerines and apples stained with strawberry pink. Some yellow pears, smooth as silk, some white grapes covered with a silver bloom and a big cluster of purple ones. When she had finished with them and had made two pyramids of these bright round shapes, she stood away to get the effect—and it really was most curious. For the dark table seemed to melt into the dusky light and the glass dish and the blue bowl to float in the air.

More important than any happening is the way Bertha sees the pear tree, which Mansfield used as a symbol of the unawakened woman.

> . . . there was a tall, slender pear tree in the fullest, richest bloom; it stood perfect, as though becalmed against the jade-green sky. Bertha couldn't help feeling, even from this distance, that it had not a single bud or a faded petal. Down below . . . a grey cat, dragging its belly, crept across the lawn, and a black one, its shadow, tailed after.

The writer has many devices at hand to create his moods: imagery; symbolism; choice of words and letter sounds; repetition of words, phrases, and sentences; sentence structure. Tone results from a combination of such devices. It is no single thing but a kind of aura, an emotional aura, related to that undefinable magic quality of a truly excellent story.

Start Writing!

1. Present a commonplace event (perhaps a visit to a super-market) in an opening paragraph that sets the tone in two of three ways: brooding, matter-of-fact, or dreamlike.
2. Introduce a usually happy event (a birthday party or picnic) in such a manner that the reader is warned that it will, or may, end in disaster.
3. Describe an athletic event in tight muscular prose that conveys the rigors and rhythms of the event.

Suggested Reading

Nathaniel Benchley, *The Hunter's Moon* (Boston: Little, Brown, 1972).

Truman Capote, *Selected Writings of Truman Capote* (New York: Random House, 1963).

Shirley Jackson, *The Magic of Shirley Jackson* (New York: Farrar, Straus & Giroux, 1966).

Katherine Mansfield, *Short Stories by Katherine Mansfield* (New York: Knopf, 1937).

Carson McCullers, *Collected Short Stories* (New York: Houghton Mifflin, 1955).

Robert Nathan, *The Elixir* (New York: Knopf, 1971).

Edna O'Brien, *Night* (New York: Knopf, 1973).

Sylvia Plath, *The Bell Jar* (New York: Harper & Row 1971).

Edgar Allan Poe, *Complete Stories and Poems* (New York: Doubleday, 1966).

Eudora Welty, *Wide Net and Other Stories* (Harcourt Brace Jovanovich, 1943).

11

Style

Style is the way a person does something, the way he dresses, walks, smokes a cigarette, handles a situation, drives a car, speaks. When we say that a person has style, we mean that he has a style that is pleasing to us. Actually every person has a style of his own.

Style is the way a writer writes. Some of it he has acquired during his young reading years; more of it he has developed deliberately during his writing years. No one is born with it. One is born, so it seems, with a flair for words or a sense of words, a love and respect for language, but certainly William Faulkner was not born with his unique style. He adapted his style to himself, his way of thinking, and his subject matter.

INDIVIDUALITY

There are many kinds of styles and many variations of them. We think of James Thurber's and Robert Benchley's styles as humorous; yet they are in no way similar. Hemingway and Flannery O'Connor have a terse and economical style, yet each is recognizable for his or her own way of handling words, phrases, sentences. No one would confuse the complicated styles of Henry James and William Faulkner or the precise styles of Katherine Mansfield and Katherine Anne Porter. A part of the easy identification of writers is their subject matter which cannot be separated from their style. Style does not exist for its own sake. It is the way a writer says something.

It should go without saying that a beginning writer would not seek to imitate the successful writers he admires, but the imitators, doomed from the beginning, are many. The saddest thing that can happen to a young writer by the name of Jones is to be called a new Hemingway, a new Steinbeck, or a new Faulkner. It is far better for him to be called a groping, awkward, but promising Jones. And his happiest moment should be when someone says to him, "No one but you, Jones, could have written this."

At the other extreme, the search for originality for the sake of originality may doom the writer, too. This writer faces the danger of becoming merely a stylist, which is nothing. Again, a writer has to write about something; he must have something to say.

An excellent example of a writer's ability to combine style and subject matter is this paragraph from Stephen Vincent Benét's "The Devil and Daniel Webster."

> You see, for a while, he was the biggest man in the country. He never got to be President, but he was the biggest man. There were thousands that trusted in him right next to God Almighty, and they told stories about him and all the things that belonged to him that were like the stories of patriarchs and such. They said when he stood up to speak, stars and stripes came right out in the sky, and once he spoke against a river and made it sink into the ground. They said, when he walked the woods with his fishing rod, Killall, the trout, would jump out of the streams right into his pockets, for they knew it was no use putting up a fight against him; and, when he argued a case, he could turn on the harps of the blessed and the shaking of the earth underground.*

RESPECT FOR LANGUAGE

Style comes first from the writer's lifelong love affair with language. He is forever doing something with words because he can't leave them alone. And he improves his style as he increases his respect for language.

* From *Selected Works of Stephen Vincent Benét*, Holt, Rinehart & Winston. Copyright 1936 by The Curtis Publishing Company. Quoted by permission of Brandt and Brandt.

The writer who loves and admires language does not—in his haste to say something—allow himself to use clichés, hackneyed phrases, abstractions, and broad generalities nor any but the exact word for what he wishes to express. Nor does he fall into the sloppy use of "journalese," "governmentese," and pseudoscientific terms.

To get out of the habit of thinking symbolically in clichés, the writer has to look at the things around him as if he were seeing them for the first time, as if he had been born (*sic*) yesterday.

"White as snow" says the advertiser about a pile of sheets washed by his detergent. This cliché has no meaning. There are many shades of white; there are many shades of snow. More important, the reader or listener no longer responds to the image, for he has seen or heard it too often. It has become a single word, whiteasnow.

The writer must look at the word "white" and ask himself what meaning the word has for him. A good practice for the writer is to make a list of the colors and try to see them as if he had never seen them before. What to him is blue? Red? Not the sky, not blood. And what is black?

He should also find his own fresh similes for the worn-out "thin as a rail," "sharp as a tack," "handsome as a Greek god," "happy as a lark," and the many other similes and metaphors that have become single words, thus meaningless, through overuse. The careless poet likes to write about a girl with the voice of a nightingale though neither he nor his readers have ever seen or heard a nightingale and wouldn't recognize the bird if they did hear one. The reader responds to a fresh figure of speech as well as to the impact of the single, well-selected word. "Still as mountains with morning drawn up in their valleys," says Phyllis Roberts in her story "Hero."

Hackneyed language includes clichés and many phrases which have simply been overused. The latter can give the writer more trouble than clichés, for clichés are more easily recognized and eliminated. Hackneyed phrases consist of combinations of quite respectable words: golden and sunset, engaging and grin, infectious and smile, cruel and April. It is not the word itself but the combination of two of them that has become boring. A list of these would be endless; it is the writer's love for language that will rid him of winding paths, gentle breezes, pale moons, breathing deeply, high shrill voices, silhouettes against the sky, freezing with fear, proud possessors, catching somebody's eye, and blinding flashes.

The overuse of abstractions and glittering generalities is likely to be a weakness of the young writer, who is inclined to say "Life is . . . ," "Love is . . . ," "Courage is . . . ." These are of course good theme subjects, but effective writers will use specific and concrete words that will imply life or courage or love or justice. The specific story of what happened to Anne Frank is worth a thousand treatises on the subject of justice. Jesus Christ told the simple story of the Good Samaritan; he did not expound on the subject of brotherly love.

It is easy to avoid abstractions and generalities if the writer will look at a person or a thing with his senses rather than with his intellect. He must learn to see, hear, smell, and touch the thing or the person. The lazy writer who does not love language will not learn this. It is easier to generalize than to be specific.

Katherine Anne Porter, in love with language for about seventy years, said this about it in *McCall's*, August, 1965:

> There is a natural human speech which is the speech of litera-
> ture, of human beings. . . . It isn't from the gutter, and it isn't
> exalted. It isn't Pentagonese or Madison Avenue, or Freudian jar-
> gon . . . or the steerage-bilge school of criticism—it is the daily
> human speech of those who love and respect their mother tongue
> and learn to speak it correctly. . . . I can't understand why
> people think they can get through life on a vocabulary of three
> hundred and fifty words—we have such a marvelous, rich lan-
> guage, and I don't know why we are so tolerant of the dull minds
> who try to destroy it. . . .

POINTS TO REMEMBER

Developing one's style is almost synonymous with rewriting. The French writer Colette, whose writing seems facile, often spent an entire day on a single page of a short story. Flaubert needed seven years to write *Madame Bovary*. It is said of him—apocryphally, as of other writers—that he spent the morning putting in a comma and the afternoon taking it out.

However, since vitality is the most important factor in writing, the writer must revise intelligently. He must not worry his story into a state of meatlessness.

Style may tend to simplicity or to richness, but whichever it is, it is not burdened by superfluous modifiers. Complex as Faulkner's style is, it is not weakened by redundant adjectives and adverbs. Most beginning writers err on the side of overusing adjectives and adverbs: they use a modifier to prop up a weak noun or verb or to help identify an inexact noun or verb. Robert Frost said: "Nouns and verbs are pure metal; adjectives and adverbs are cheaper ore. . . . Death to the adjective!" One of my students wrote this: "Mark's lips were two thin straight lines. He pounded his fist on the table. 'Everything you've said here is a lie,' he said confidently." The "confidently" is, of course, superfluous. The description, the narration, and the line of dialogue have already expressed Mark's confidence in what he is saying. A good weekly exercise for a writer with a modifier problem is to write a 300-word incident without using any adjectives or adverbs, forcing his nouns and verbs to carry the entire burden.

Apologetic phrases, such as "it seems," "it looked as if," "so to speak," also weaken style. This is the side of the coin whose other face is the glittering generality. The timid writer, afraid of his strong statement, tries to temper it with one of these weakening phrases. Other weakeners are participial phrases and an overuse of the passive voice and the long Latin derivative.

The writer should beware the tendency of many Hemingway imitators to confuse simplicity with vacuity and the temptation of many Wolfe imitators to confuse richness with thickness.

An often-quoted verse written by the ubiquitous "Anon" says:

> The written word
> Should be clean as bone
> Clear as light
> Firm as stone

    Two words are not
    As good as one.

This concept can be defended whatever style the writer has found to be his own. Even for the ornate style, rich in imagery and symbolism, the word itself should be clean, clear, firm. No one has ever made a strong case against clarity.

Start Writing!

1. Write a poem or a 300-word essay without using *any* modifiers.
2. Describe a picture which you have never seen but would like to have in your house.
3. In one or more paragraphs tell where you would most like to have your house of all the places in the world. Do not describe the house; just tell about the place.
4. Describe two bedrooms: the one you occupied as a child and one that reveals the personality of someone you know.
5. The euphony of your writing depends on the sensitivity of your ear. Words have weight, sound, appearance.
   a. List ten words that sound beautiful to you, regardless of meaning.
   b. List ten words that sound ugly to you, regardless of meaning.
   c. List ten words that sound heavy to you.
   d. List ten words that sound light to you.
6. Write a two-page or page-and-a-half description of a scene of violence.
7. Writers, particularly poets, are aware of the weakness of abstractions. How would you express in concrete ways the following abstract words: freedom, happiness, equality, hope, mercy, evil, justice, progress, ambition, faith?

Suggested Reading

Conrad Aiken, *Short Stories* (Freeport, New York: Books for Libraries).

Truman Capote, *Selected Writings of Truman Capote* (New York: Random House, 1963).

William Faulkner, *Collected Stories* (New York: Random House, 1950).

Ernest Hemingway, *Short Stories of Ernest Hemingway* (New York: Scribner's, 1938).

Rona Jaffe, *The Other Woman* (New York: Morrow, 1972).

D.H. Lawrence, *The Complete Short Stories of D.H. Lawrence* (3 vols.) (New York: Viking, 1961).

Wright Morris, *Wright Morris: A Reader* (New York: Harper & Row, 1970).

Anais Nin, *Under a Glass Bell* (Chicago: Swallow Press, 1968).

Philip Roth, *The Breast* (New York: Bantam Books, 1973).

Irwin Shaw, *Selected Short Stories* (New York: Random House, 1967).

Jesse Stuart, *The Land Beyond the River* (New York: McGraw-Hill, 1973).

Eudora Welty, *Losing Battles* (New York: Random House, 1970).

12

Nonfiction: Magazine Essays and Articles

The essay, formal or informal, implies a certain literary quality. The formal essay, once a familiar form in almost all magazines, has survived in the publications specializing in literature and other arts, political science, history, foreign affairs, and so on. The informal essay has a large market, for it is in demand by quality and commercial magazines. The magazine article, sometimes considered identical with the informal essay, has its largest market in the commercial magazines.

ESSAYS

The formal and the informal essay differ in tone, style, and the author's purpose.

The Formal Essay

The tone of the formal essay is scholarly; the style, literary; and the writer's purpose, to interest a select group of readers in some unexplored area of his subject. The formal essay requires exceptional erudition and reputation on the part of the writer.

The Informal Essay

Magazine editors welcome informal essays from any source if the subjects are pertinent and the writing has quality. The informal essay is conversational in style, and its subject is something that people are likely to be talking about. In common with the formal essay, it is more likely to deal with an abstract idea than with facts and figures.

The market for the informal essay is about the same as that for the quality story. The range of style and tone is wide: it may be satirical or serious and provocative, or humorous and provocative. It can be controversial. Subject matter is unlimited.

The structure of the informal essay is similar to that of fiction. It has a line of suspense that keeps the reader interested enough to finish it. Like the short story, it does not just ramble along, but rises to a kind of climax and solution. It has an overall problem, and it has a theme. Unlike fiction, it must have a thesis. The thesis is what the writer believes to be true and endeavors to prove. It may be explicitly stated or it may be implied.

ARTICLES

The magazine article has in common with the informal essay an extensive readership and unlimited subject material. Both forms have themes and theses, and both follow the same structural plan. The differences between them are the tone, which in the magazine article is likely to be "chatty" and in the essay conversational, and the method of handling the subject matter. Whereas the subject of the essay tends toward abstraction, the subject of the magazine article is concerned more with facts and figures and data of all kinds. A magazine article about a person is generally a feature story, rather than a story that illustrates an abstraction.

Commercial magazines publish both the informal essay and the article. In one issue of *Esquire*, for example, Brock Brower wrote what may be labeled an informal essay. The title is "Forty Thoughts on Turning Forty." The problems of becoming forty years old make up the thesis, and the material used is subservient to the thesis. In another issue of *Esquire*, Grace Lichtenstein wrote what may be labeled an article. The title is "A Nation of Fat Heads." The thesis is presented by the editor and reads: "Why are Irwin Stillman, Robert Atkins, Jack La Lanne, Teddy Kennedy, Totie Fields, David Reuben, Shelley Winters, Dick Gregory, you, us, seventy-nine million other Americans, and God and his angels so obsessed with dieting?" The important features of this article are the facts about the diet compulsion and the accumulation of data which gives the reader an impression of complete authority.

Title

The titles of magazine articles are of primary importance, for they must catch the attention of the busy reader who quickly leafs through the magazine, stopping only for something that immediately interests him. The writer's name may stop him—this is one reason publishers are compelled to use some name writers in every issue. But even more important is the title. Lichtenstein's title "A Nation of Fat Heads" is unbeatable. It would seize the attention of men, women, and young readers.

Brock Brower's title "Forty Thoughts on Turning Forty" would appeal to the majority of *Esquire's* readership. Readers would be attracted by such titles as "Can You Afford to Have Teeth?" by Gerald Astor and "Death as a Career" written for *Harper's* by Studs Terkel. Another kind of reader would want to read "How Sight Becomes Insight" by Annie Dillard, also in *Harper's*.

Opening Paragraph

Second in importance to the title is the opening paragraph, both in the magazine article and in the informal essay. The writer uses every trick he knows to involve the reader in his first paragraph, for he knows that doing this in the second paragraph is too late. He uses anecdotes, examples, allusions, dialogue, and whatever he believes will capture and keep his reader.

Grace Lichtenstein uses a familiar trick, the second person pronoun, to involve her readers in the first paragraph of "A Nation of Fat Heads."

> How much have you lost lately? I bet you know—and I bet you might not have known a few years ago. I bet you know now because you stepped on the scale first thing this morning, before you brushed your teeth. I bet you feel the fires of hell licking at your heels every time you pop a Hershey's Kiss into your mouth. I bet just the *thought* of cottage cheese makes you feel pounds lighter.*

Betty Moffitt in the *Ladies' Home Journal*, April, 1974, writes a brief action paragraph to open her article. "The 11-year-old girl rushed into the kitchen. 'Mom! Mom!' she called out breathlessly, 'I'm going to be a tennis player.'" The title of the article is "My Daughter Billie Jean."

Development

Lichtenstein deveolps her article on dieters logically. She states her premise, then presents the overall picture of what she calls our number-one participatory sport.

This paragraph is followed by quotes from such famous people as Mike Douglas, Shelley Winters, and Senator Kennedy. The author then gives impressive statistics on the numbers of dieters and the amount of money involved in the diet-food market, reducing salons, health spas, and the conglomerate called Weight Watchers.

Several long paragraphs are given to a description of the books which the writer calls the heart of the new diet consciousness. She mentions first Joe Bonomo's little twenty-five-cent calorie counter of the fifties, then the taller book which announced that calories didn't count, and the biggest one of all, *Dr. Atkins' Diet Revolution*.

Much of the article is a pro-con discussion of the methods advocated by Dr. Atkins, Dr. Irwin Stillman, and Jean Nidetch of Weight Watchers.

The concluding seven paragraphs of the article have to do with

* *Esquire*, August, 1973.

the most serious aspect of the subject: the various implications of diet consciousness such as the loss of our sense of proportion about food, the psychic damage we do to our self-images, and an actual disease brought on by deliberate self-starvation.

Research

Lichtenstein did not sit down at her desk and pull her facts and figures out of her imagination. She did a patient, thorough job of research, the most important element in nonfiction writing.

The article itself is probably the merest tip of the iceberg emerging from the vast amount of reading and inquiring demanded by such a study. Light and irreverent in tone as it often is, this article is a result of comprehensive library and people research. Tracking down busy people and obtaining quotes from them requires endless patience, tact, and insight.

More nonfiction articles are rejected for inadequate research than for bad writing; unless all the facts and examples that defend the writer's thesis are presented the writing itself has no value.

Every article is researched in a different way, but there are basic steps. Step one is at the library's card index file and *Books in Print*. Lichtenstein would have checked the file under the headings of diet and nutrition, recording the author and title of books to which she might wish to refer.

Step two is a prolonged visit to the *Reader's Guide to Periodical Literature* and other indexes. For an article like Lichtenstein's, these sources are more important than the card index. From the *Guide*, for example, the writer can learn what has already been published by the magazines about a subject and can get information that is too recent for books. The *Guide* lists magazine articles by subject and by author's name, with the date of publication. Not only can the writer determine what has been published about his subject, but he can also read the pertinent articles in the library.

Another source Lichtenstein would have found useful is *The New York Times Index*. Recorded on microfilm are indexed news stories on the thousands of subjects that have appeared in *The*

Times. Perhaps from this source alone she would have found the material she needed for the historical part of her essay.

Also from these three library sources she could have gotten the names, occupations, and points of view of some of the people she needed to interview. And to know more about these people before she interviewed them, she could have looked for them in *Who's Who* and in the many variations, according to professions, on *Who's Who*.

Step three is the interview with the experts and the authorities. This is easy enough for a celebrated writer who has only to dial a number and arrange an interview. For the less renowned, it is better to write a brief letter, stating clearly what the writer wants to discuss with the expert. The busier the expert, the more likely he is to agree to the interview. If the expert is too far away to be interviewed, the writer can ask by letter a few specific questions that will give him the information he needs. He can also give the expert his phone number and ask to be called collect.

The interview itself is a work of art, and the nonfiction writer should endeavor to master it. He must know enough about his subject to ask questions that the expert will be delighted to answer. He must suppress any desire he has to impress the expert with his knowledge. To get information the expert will not be delighted to give, he must wait until he can word his questions casually and if possible keep his notebook out of sight. He should try to get all of his information in one interview.

With the information he now has, the writer is prepared to query the magazine editors. He should not waste time writing his article until he has interested an editor. Most editors like to see a complete outline, a page or two showing the author's writing style, and a little biographical data. (Read appendix I on preparing the manuscript.) The writer, if he sends his outline to a reputable magazine, need not worry that someone is going to steal his idea.

Accuracy

In the success of a nonfiction article, accuracy is just as important as adequate research. Accuracy means not only spelling names and identifying people correctly, but also telling the story without distortions such as quoting out of context, misquoting, exaggerating, or sacrificing truth to make a point. There is a fine line between selecting the right data to expound a thesis and twisting the data, but the fine line must be drawn by the serious nonfiction writer.

Start Writing!

1. The most creative person is the one on whom nothing is lost. Creative people are lovers of the qualities of things; they wish to experience life in its fullest sense. This is the essence of the creative temper. What have you experienced lately in the fullest sense? Write an informal essay about it.

2. "No more can come out of a writer than has gone into him through his environment," says Dr. Frederick Schorer. "The power of the writer is not separate from the power of the moment in which he is living. The meagreness of twentieth century writing is caused by a world that provides inadequate experience." Write a short essay about this whether you agree or disagree.

3. The nonfiction writer must be able to handle other people's ideas with reason and logic. Write a few paragraphs analyzing the following quotation from Dr. Frank Barron: "The creative man may be both naive and knowledgeable, being at home equally to primitive symbolism and to rigorous logic. He is both more primitive and more cultured, more destructive and more constructive, occasionally crazier and yet adamantly saner than the average person."

4. Write an informal essay on Maeterlinck's statement: "The manner in which the hours of freedom are spent, no less than labor and war, determines the moral worth of a nation."

5. What possible events in your life are likely to shake you up the most? Name three. Write several paragraphs about one.

6. Songwriter Dory Previn says, "One critic said I write songs about things that should be left unsaid. I don't think anything needs to be left unsaid about the human condition." Discuss this in a short essay.

7. An informal journal helps the writer maintain a daily writing habit. Keep a journal for thirty days recording ideas, images, new insights. Avoid a mere narration of activities. Record, rather, what the activities mean to you.

8. The easiest way to write a magazine article is the question-and-answer interview, for which you prepare the questions. Write a five-minute (three typewritten pages) interview with a member of your family (or with yourself).

STRUCTURE OF NONFICTION

Generally speaking, a writer will start with an appealing and compelling first paragraph which may or may not include his thesis statement. By the second paragraph, he will have made his statement, the opinion or concept which he will then set out to prove. The rest of the article (except for a concluding paragraph) will present the evidence of his statement.

Development of Thesis Statement

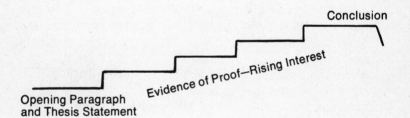

Conclusion

Evidence of Proof—Rising Interest

Opening Paragraph
and Thesis Statement

Examples of Thesis Statements

1. The proposed Equal Rights Amendment would actually create hardships for nonprofessional women.

2. Large tax deductions for oil companies are beneficial to the national economy in the long run.
3. A federal gun-control law is unnecessary since state and local laws, if enforced, would be sufficient.
4. Maintaining impoverished mothers on relief costs more than government funded child-care centers which would free them to find jobs (and pay their share of income taxes).

Start Writing!

1. Select one thesis statement from the above and write an opening paragraph to introduce it.
2. Make an outline, paragraph by paragraph, of the material that is evidence for the truth of your thesis statement.
3. Write the concluding paragraph.
4. Decide on a title for your article or essay.

13

Booklength Nonfiction

One advantage booklength nonfiction has over the novel is longevity. It has a five to one chance of outlasting a novel published during the same year.

The second advantage is to the writer's ego. It is generally accepted that the books most profoundly affecting our society are not fiction. A poll taken by the *Saturday Review* in a recent year indicated that during the preceding forty years the truly important books were concerned with economics, sociology, war, sex, natural resources, psychology, sciences, religion, and morality. The few influential novels included Steinbeck's *The Grapes of Wrath*, Huxley's *Brave New World*, Orwell's *1984*, and Hemingway's *For Whom the Bell Tolls*, novels having strong themes dealing with the human condition.

SUBJECT

Broadly, nonfiction reflects current events. It was natural that in 1964, following the assassination of President Kennedy, the leading titles were Kennedy books and books dealing with the presidency. In 1963 readers of nonfiction were interested in Kennedy books and in James Baldwin's *The Fire Next Time*, a black's point of view on race problems.

Other booklength nonfiction reflecting the public's interest in current events includes books dealing with the environment, Indian problems, governmental and economic crises, and the bicentennial of the American Revolution. Examples are John Kenneth Galbraith's *Economics and the Public Purpose*, Alvin Toffler's *Future Shock*, and Dee Brown's *Bury My Heart at Wounded Knee: An Indian History of the American West*.

Booklength nonfiction that frequently makes the best-seller lists is about political leaders of any country or any era. Hitler continues to attract wide readership with such books as *The Mind of Adolf Hitler* by Walter C. Langer (Basic Books, New York, 1972) and *The Twelve-Year Reich: A Social History of Nazi Germany* by Richard Grunberger (Holt, Rinehart & Winston, New York, 1971).

Books of personal reminiscence such as Lillian Hellman's *Pentimento: A Book of Portraits* and the endless volumes on life in the White House often reach the best-seller lists.

The two years following the death of President Roosevelt in 1945 saw the publication of many Roosevelt books, although the leading nonfiction title of 1945, the war's end, was Ernie Pyle's *Brave Men*. Books dealing with the war were, of course, best sellers from 1941 to 1945. Hitler's *Mein Kampf* headed the list of nonfiction in 1939. In 1936 John Gunther began his long series of "inside" books with *Inside Europe*.

Biography and autobiography are ceaselessly interesting to writers and readers of nonfiction, whether the subjects are of genuine stature or only of transitional fame. Successful books in this field have included Anita Loos's *A Girl Like I*, Colette's *Mémoires*, John F. Kennedy's *Profiles in Courage*, Bernard Baruch's *My Own Story*, Moss Hart's *Act One*, Frederic Morton's *The Rothschilds*, Louis Nizer's *My Life In Court*, and the many biographical studies of John F. Kennedy.

Religious and other kinds of inspirational books are a strong, perhaps the strongest, contributing factor to the longevity of nonfiction. The Bible and *The Prophet* are apparently immortal. The Jerusalem Bible and the New English Bible gave additional impetus to Bible-buying during the past decade.

Inspirational nonfiction remains on best-seller lists year after year: *The Power of Positive Thinking, A Guide to Confident Living,* and *Stay Alive All of Your Life* by Norman Vincent Peale; Joshua Liebman's *Peace of Mind* and Fulton J. Sheen's *Peace of Soul;* Peter Marshall's sermons and prayers; Fulton Oursler's *The Greatest Story Ever Told.* Dale Carnegie had a continuing success with *How to Win Friends and Influence People.*

Titles like *Wake Up and Live, Live Alone and Like It, Sex and the Single Girl,* and *I'm OK—You're OK* are almost guarantees in themselves that readers will buy the books.

The American mind is essentially curious, about its own mind, other people's minds, other people's manners and mores; about its surroundings (seas, mountains, outer space); about the very rich and the very poor; about the inner sanctum (anywhere or anyone's); about the successful and the beautiful, the high and the mighty on its way up or on its way down; about the unique, the daring, the "first-to." It is as interested in the kidnapping of Lindbergh's son as it is in Lindbergh's achievement in the air. It likes to read Rachel Carson's *Silent Spring* and *The Sea Around Us;* it also likes to read about Bob Hope in Russia.

A part of the American mind is not only curious, but educable. This mind accounts for the long, lasting list of books printed and reprinted in all fields of learning: science, history, literature, economics, mathematics. It is not possible even to list the topics of these books, but I have in mind such titles as Gunnar Myrdal's *An American Dilemma,* Gilbert Ryle's *The Concept of Mind,* Charles Beard's *An Economic Interpretation of the Constitution,* Franz Boas's *Anthropology and Modern Life,* David Riesman's *The Lonely Crowd,* Albert Einstein's *The Meaning of Relativity.*

Still another part of the American mind likes to be able to do things. "Novelty" books are published by the millions to satisfy this part of the national mind: books on hobbies, cooking, gardening, homemaking, carpentry, the long, inexhaustible list of "how-to" books from *How to Read a Book* to *How to Build a Castle in Spain.*

RELATION TO OTHER FORMS

In the field of current events the writer has to compete with the nonwriter, for it is the man and the event that are important for the moment to the reader. *Mein Kampf* was a styleless monstrosity, written by a nonwriter, Adolf Hitler. Similarly, many books are written at times of crisis by nonwriters or by ghostwriters. These latter are the many "as-told-to" books that interest the public only as long as the man and his moment endure.

In specialized books the writer's competitor is the expert, who may not be a great writer (he may even be a nonwriter) but whose authority in his field is unquestionable. He has spent perhaps half a lifetime earning the right to be an authority in anthropology, philosophy, mathematics, or in a lesser field, such as landscape gardening or bonsai. The many handbooks and outlines on specific subjects are, of course, written by experts who can write.

In biography, a most lucrative branch of nonfiction writing, the beginning writer is in competition with the expert who is also a well-trained writer. The biographer knows not only where and how to find his material but how to use it to produce a readable, interesting book that is also acceptable to the other authorities on his subject.

Biography, in common with fiction, needs a theme, a structure that will carry suspense, a proper use of time, a careful use of details. Like the novelist, the biographer must find the moments of decision in the life of his subject that make the subject worth writing about. And like the novelist, he must be able to make his characters "come off" as human beings. All of this must be achieved in spite of the limitations of truth, facts, and objectivity. Thus the biographer carries a double burden: He must write nonfiction that reads like fiction.

The structure of booklength nonfiction in general has much in common with the novel: conflicts and problems that must be solved, crises that must be met, a theme that is carried along with the events, a chronological or a logical use of time, perhaps flashbacks, all reaching a climax of a kind and a resolution, the total achieving a unity of effect demanded of the novel.

STRUCTURE

A basic structural design underlies every kind of writing, although the novelist may deviate from it in various ways. The nonfiction writer must determine the shape of his work and then construct it. He needs to prepare a blueprint or a complete outline. Most nonfiction works (not necessarily biographies) present a major thesis and some minor ones. Every chapter and every paragraph of the book will be used to prove, explain, substantiate, or illustrate those theses. Hence the need for a blueprint that will keep the writer from wandering off to another structure.

The Lonely Crowd: A Study of the Changing American Character, written by David Riesman with Nathan Glazer and Reuel Denney, is an example of a perfectly designed work of nonfiction.

An outline of the book would show that it falls into three major parts, logically connected: part one, character; part two, politics; and part three, autonomy. The authors then divide the first part into seven chapters whose titles indicate that they will define, explain, give examples of, and interpret the American social character. Titles of chapters in the second part show that the relationship between politics and social character is being explored; chapter titles in the third part relate the changing social character to autonomy in American life.

Each chapter is then subdivided into two or three sections, which in turn are divided into smaller titled parts. Chapter thirteen, for example, reads like this:

False Personalization: Obstacles to Autonomy in Work

I. Cultural Definitions of Work
II. Glamorizers, Featherbedders, Indispensables
    White-collar personalization: toward glamor
    The conversation of the classes: factory model
    The club of indispensables
III. The Overpersonalized Society
    The automat versus the glad hand

In the first paragraph of the first chapter, the authors explain clearly what the book is about.

> This is a book about social character and about the differences in social character between men of different regions, eras, and groups. It considers the ways in which different social character types, once they are formed at the knee of society, are then deployed in the work, play, politics, and child-rearing activities of society. More particularly, it is about the way in which one kind of social character, which dominated America in the nineteenth century, is gradually being replaced by a social character of quite a different sort. Just why this happened; how it happened; what are its consequences in some major areas of life; this is the subject of this book.*

The thesis of *The Lonely Crowd* is that a change is visible in the character of the American people, that formerly our society was dominated by "inner-directed" men, men who accepted or represented adult authority, the pioneers, the individualists; that now the tendency is toward domination by "other-directed" men, or those whose character is formed by the examples of their peers; that this trend is leading to an adjustment to society, depriving men of their individual automony.

The book has related minor theses, all of which contribute directly to the main thesis.

In addition to the subject matter the writer's style makes his work appealing to many readers rather than to a limited group and gives it the longevity of a book like *The Lonely Crowd*. A more pedantic kind of writer might have presented the same subject matter in the jargon of his profession that repels readers. The authors of *The Lonely Crowd* use the specialized vocabulary sparingly and define it clearly.

In nonfiction writing, clarity must take precedence over the writer's desire to have an original or complex style, for the reader is seeking information and revelation first. Communication between writer and reader is primary. Muddiness of style halts communication, and muddiness comes from careless syntax, sloppy word selection, jargon, the use of foreign words for which there are adequate English ones, the overuse of the long Latin derivative

* David Riesman, *The Lonely Crowd* (New Haven, Conn.: Yale University Press, 1950).

because it sounds "fancier" than the Anglo-Saxon one, and the overuse of modifiers and the passive voice.

An effect of objectivity is also essential to good nonfiction. Although the writer has a thesis and will surely reach some conclusions about it, the bulk of the work will give the reader the feeling that the writer is presenting his material objectively.

Finally, the total nonfiction work must carry an overtone of authority. The reader must sense that the writer has given his subject the research and study the subject deserves. It is not enough for the writer to state in a preface his qualifications for writing about the changing character of the American people. The work itself must convince the reader that the writer knows what he is talking about, that he can be trusted, and that his opinions and judgments are valid. This sense of authority is essential to the magazine article; it is doubly essential to booklength nonfiction.

Suggested Reading

Robert Atkins, *Dr. Atkins' Diet Revolution: The High Calorie Way to Stay Thin Forever* (New York: McKay, 1972).

Alex Comfort, *The Joy of Sex* (New York: Crown, 1972).

Thomas Harris, *I'm OK—You're OK: A Practical Guide to Transactional Analysis* (New York: Harper & Row, 1969).

Joseph Lash, *Eleanor: The Years Alone* (New York: Norton, 1972).

Vance Packard, *A Nation of Strangers* (New York: McKay, 1972).

Colin Simpson, *The Lusitania* (Boston: Little, Brown, 1973).

Adam Smith, *Supermoney* (New York: Random House, 1972).

14

The Pains of Revision

One of the differences between the amateur and the professional writer is the latter's willingness to revise and to rewrite, to cut and throw away, however painful and bloodletting the operation may be.

Revision of both fiction and nonfiction includes two processes: reorganization of material, if necessary, and a long look at paragraphs, sentences, and words.

Revisions of fictional works demand certain tests: of the beginning of the story, its progress toward the climax, the uses of time, the ending, the immediacy, the single effect, and the title itself. Questions must be answered: Does the story have a theme. Is it about something? Are the point of view and focus consistent? Are the characters believably developed or revealed? Is the dialogue natural?

THE BEGINNING

To test the beginning of a story, the writer asks himself if he has started the story too soon, too late, or at exactly the right time. The rambling, leisurely beginning of a Henry James or a Hawthorne story is not acceptable today. On the other hand, starting a story too close to the climax may result in the omission of information necessary to the reader. The writer has to seize his

111

reader with the first paragraph or two, and it is worth his time to rewrite his introduction as many times as he finds it necessary. These are the paragraphs that tell the reader to stop and listen to what the writer has to say. A study of the first paragraphs of Flaubert's stories and novels is a worthy exercise. There is no single right way to begin a story, but any beginning must engage the reader through a specific character, a specific incident, a specific conversation, or a specific mood. Flannery O'Connor engaged the reader of "A Good Man Is Hard to Find" by introducing the maniac killer through a newspaper report at the beginning of the story. The reader doesn't know what is going to happen, but he can be certain that O'Connor will make use of this character.

THE TRANSITION

When he has tested his beginning, the writer looks at his transitions. Do they lead from one part of the story smoothly into the next, or do they require too big a jump on the part of the reader? When the writer uses flashbacks, he must examine his transitions with particular care. It must be clear, though imperceptible to the reader, that the writer is flashing back, then returning to the present time.

An interesting use of time for every transition is F. Scott Fitzgerald's "The Jelly-Bean." Badly used, this technique of using time sequences can be stilted and boring, but Fitzgerald was a master of it. The fourteen transitions in this long story are as follows:

Jim was born . . .
He became fifteen . . .
He became eighteen . . .
When the war was over . . .
In the twilight of one April evening . . .
Back in the days when . . .
When the dusk had thickened . . .
At nine-thirty . . .
So ten o'clock found Jelly-Bean . . .
He had been there half an hour . . .

At twelve o'clock . . .
A bleak room echoed all day . . .
In the sunshine of three o'clock . . .
The street was hot at three and still hotter at four . . .

THE STRUCTURE

The writer then tests the rest of his story for structure. Does everything in it lead inevitably, yet unpredictably, to the conclusion? Is the story paced right, or does it go on monotonously in the same tone and rhythm? Every detail of "A Good Man Is Hard to Find," including the color of the son's shirt, is an indispensable part of the story. The fact that the grandmother brought her cat on the trip leads directly to the mass murder in the second part of the story. The pacing, too, is exactly right. When the action became unbearable, O'Connor stopped for a moment of important reflection, then plunged back into what was happening. The beginning writer must be careful to control his action; too long a reflection or description may lose the reader.

The writer must check his story for immediacy. Does it seem to be taking place before the reader's eyes, or does it seem remote? If it seems remote, the writer may have too little dialogue, too much narrative in the past perfect tense, too much recall on the part of the protagonist, or too much exposition.

To test the single effect of a short story or the unified effect of a novel, the writer has to take the seat of the reader. When he finishes reading the story, does he feel what the writer wanted him to feel and conclude what the writer wanted him to conclude?

THE COMPOSITION

When the writer is satisfied that his story is right, he goes back to examine his paragraphs, sentences, words. At this point he must avoid two extremes: careless word selection and paragraphing and overpolishing to the death of his writing.

He should keep in mind that the paragraph is not just a group of sentences; it is a group of sentences that form a unit, a unit that adds a new thought to the story. It may be only one sentence, or if the writer is William Faulkner, it may be three pages long. Dialogue is paragraphed as one speaker takes the conversation from another.

The fiction writer has more freedom with sentence structure than the nonfiction writer. For example, fragments and ellipses may be necessary to his style or to the story. The nonfiction writer has little reason to use any but the well-structured sentence, which Winston Churchill considered a noble thing.

Both kinds of writers have a responsibility to the word. George Orwell set down a few of his own rules for it: "Never use a metaphor or an image you have seen in print. Never use a long word when a short one will do as well. Avoid foreign words for which there are equivalents in your own language. Never use four words when one is sufficient. . . . Be able to break all these rules."*

The writer should check his story for the exact word. In his first draft he may have hastily or lazily used words that only approximate his meaning instead of expressing it precisely.

He should take a long look at his modifiers. Has he used adjectives to give force to weak nouns? Has he used adverbs to give vitality to dull verbs?

He should make certain he has avoided clichés, phrases that have been used so often they might be written as one word: blindingflash, likeaGreekgod, highshrillvoice, caughthiseye, and so on.

He should test his dialogue for stilted writing by reading it aloud or by listening to it read aloud. Perhaps it has too many "He saids." Very often an entire page of dialogue will require no "He saids." Perhaps he has used too many synonyms for "He said" merely to avoid the repetition. Synonyms are worse. The word "said" is almost invisible. In dialogue the writer should avoid the inverted "Said he," or "Said Mrs. Hutch." (This old-fashioned inverted form is occasionally used now for a humorous effect.)

Finally, the writer will examine his writing for errors in grammar, syntax, punctuation, and spelling. No one has ever failed to sell

* George Orwell, "Politico and the English Language," from *Shooting an Elephant and Other Essays* (New York: Harcourt Brace Jovanovich, 1945).

a story because of a dangling modifier, but the editor expects the writing to be reasonably correct. The writer should also avoid the use of too many dots and dashes, exclamation points, and parentheses. The fact that e. e. cummings used original punctuation does not justify anyone's using it except e. e. cummings.

NONFICTION POINTS

In addition to these checking points, the nonfiction writer has some extra ones. He will check his article or book for a thesis statement. If he has written a very long article or a book, he may have some secondary theses, but he must have an overall one. The thesis statement is to the article what the single effect is to the short story. It is the writer's reason for writing the article. Transitions, chronological or logical, are even more important to him than to the fiction writer. And while the fiction writer may be content with universal truths, the nonfiction writer must be accurate with facts, quotations, and all documented material.

THE TIME TO REVISE

At what point a writer should make his revisions is a personal decision. Some writers like to write a first draft, then set it aside to cool off. After the cooling-off period, it is easier to see the weaknesses. They can revise and rewrite with just as much feeling but much less emotion. They can set up their own aesthetic distance.

Beginning writers frequently wait to revise until another person has read their stories. They also find it helpful to read their stories aloud or to listen to them read aloud. This practice can be useful if the second person is objective in his opinion or has sufficient background to give his opinion real value. Some writers, in their humility, will ask several friends to read their stories, then try to adapt all these resulting opinions to their stories. This practice has no value whatsoever.

Three books are indispensable at the time of revision: a good dictionary, a good encyclopedia, and a good thesaurus.

Bibliography

Complete lists of publishers of books, plays, short stories, fiction, and nonfiction are found in *Literary Market Place*, an annual directory published by the R. R. Bowker Company; in *1,000 Tested Money-Making Markets for Writers* by Walter G. Oleksy, published by Parker and reprinted in paperback by Barnes & Noble Books; in *The Writer* and *Writer's Digest*, two monthly magazines; and in *The Writer's Yearbook*, published by Writer's Digest, which also presents general requirements of publishers and lists of literary agents with information about their requirements. Many agents charge a fee unless the writer has a substantial publishing background. Writers interested in foreign markets may consult *Ulrich's International Periodicals Directory*. All of these reference books are available in public and college libraries. Motion picture and television markets are not included in this bibliography because they work exclusively through agents.

REFERENCE

Adburgham, Alison. *Women in Print: Writing Women and Women's Magazines from the Restoration to the Accession of Victoria*. New York: Humanities Press, Inc., 1973.

Ayer Directory of Newspapers and Periodicals. Philadelphia: N. W. Ayer and Son. Published annually.

Bartlett, John. *Bartlett's Familiar Quotations*. 14th ed. Boston: Little, Brown and Company, 1968.

Books in Print. New York: R. R. Bowker Co. Published annually.

Current Biography. New York: H. H. Wilson Co. Published monthly. Cumulated annually.

Literary Market Place: The Business Directory of American Book Publishing. New York: R. R. Bowker Co. Published annually.

Publisher's Weekly. New York: R. R. Bowker Co. Published weekly. Interim indexes published three times a year.

Readers' Guide to Periodical Literature. New York: H. H. Wilson Co. 22 issues a year. Annual and biennial cumulations.

Siemon, Frederick. *Science Fiction Story Index* (1950–1968). Chicago: American Library Association, 1971.

Ulrich's International Periodicals Directory. New York: R. R. Bowker Co. Published biennially.

Who's Who. Chicago: Marquis. Published biennially.

Writer's Market. Cincinnati: Writer's Digest. Published annually.

Writer's Yearbook. Cincinnati: Writer's Digest. Published annually.

GENERAL

Campbell, Joseph. *The Hero with a Thousand Faces*. Rev. ed. Princeton, N. J.: Princeton University Press, 1968. Reprinted in paperback.

Cary, Joyce. *Art and Reality: Ways of the Creative Process*. New York: Harper & Row, Inc., 1958. Reprinted in paperback by Doubleday (Anchor).

Cowden, Roy W., ed. *The Writer and His Craft*. Ann Arbor, Mich.: University of Michigan Press, 1956. Reprinted in paperback.

Cox, Sidney. *Indirections: For Those Who Want to Write*. New York: Alfred A. Knopf, Inc., 1947. Reprinted in paperback by Viking (Compass).

Lukacs, George. *Writer and Critic*. New York: Grosset & Dunlap, Inc., 1971.

Rehder, Jessie. *The Young Writer at Work*. New York: The Odyssey Press, 1962.

DRAMA AND FICTION

Artaud, Antonin. *The Theater and Its Double*. New York: Grove Press, 1961.

Casty, Alan. *The Dramatic Art of the Film*. New York: Harper & Row, Inc., 1971.

Esslin, Martin. *The Theatre of the Absurd*. New York: Doubleday and Co., Inc., 1961.

Fergusson, Francis. *The Human Image in Dramatic Literature*. New York: Doubleday and Co., Inc., 1957.

Forster, E. M. *Aspects of the Novel*. New York: Harcourt Brace Jovanovich, 1927. Reprinted in paperback (Harvest).

Hicks, Granville. *Literary Horizons: A Quarter Century of American Fiction*. New York: New York University Press, 1970.

Meredith, Robert, and John Fitzgerald. *The Professional Story Writer and His Art*. New York: Thomas Y. Crowell Co., 1963.
————. *Structuring Your Novel*. New York: Harper & Row, Inc., 1972.

Rowe, Kenneth T. *Write That Play*. New York: Funk & Wagnalls, 1969.

Sarton, May. "The Design of a Novel." Claremont, Calif.: Scripps College Bulletin, 1962.

Scholes, Robert. *Elements of Fiction*. New York: Oxford University Press, 1968.

Unterecker, John, ed. *Approaches to the 20th Century Novel*. New York: Thomas Y. Crowell Co., 1965.

CRITICAL ANTHOLOGIES

Bloomfield, Morton W., and R. C. Elliott, eds. *Great Plays: Sophocles to Brecht*. Rev. ed. New York: Holt, Rinehart & Winston, Inc., 1965.

Cubeta, Paul, ed. *Modern Drama for Analysis*. 3d ed. New York: Holt, Rinehart & Winston, Inc., 1962.

Ferguson, Mary Anne. *Images of Women in Literature*. Boston: Houghton Mifflin Co., 1973.

Gold, Herbert, and D. L. Stevenson, eds. *Stories of Modern America*. New York: St. Martin's Press, 1961.

Hardy, John, ed. *The Modern Talent: An Anthology of Short Stories*. New York: Holt, Rinehart & Winston, Inc., 1964.

Johnson, Willoughby, and William C. Hamlin, eds. *The Short Story*. New York: American Book Company, 1966.

Kernan, Alvin, ed. *Classics of the Modern Theater*. New York: Harcourt Brace Jovanovich, 1965.

Levin, Richard, ed. *Tragedy: Plays, Theory and Criticism*. New York: Harcourt Brace Jovanovich, 1960.

Lid, R. W., ed. *The Short Story: Classic and Contemporary*. Philadelphia: J. B. Lippincott Co., 1966.

Lovell, E. J., Jr., and W. W. Pratt, eds. *Modern Drama: An Anthology of Nine Plays*. Boston: Ginn and Co., 1963.

Ludwig, R. M., and M. B. Perry, eds. *Nine Short Novels*. Boston: D. C. Heath & Co., 1964.

Miller, James E., Jr., and Bernice Slote, eds. *The Dimensions of the Short Story*. New York: Dodd, Mead & Co., 1965.

Silverberg, Robert, ed. *The Science Fiction Hall of Fame: The Greatest Science Fiction Stories of All Time*. New York: Avon Books, 1972.

THE USE OF LANGUAGE

Flesch, Rudolf. *The Art of Readable Writing*. Rev. ed. New York: Harper & Row, Inc., 1974.

Salomon, Louis. *Semantics and Common Sense*. New York: Holt, Rinehart & Winston, Inc., 1966.

Shaw, Harry. *Writing and Rewriting*. New York: Harper & Row, Inc., 1973.

Strunk, William, Jr., and E. B. White. *Elements of Style*. New York: Crowell Collier & Macmillan, Inc., 1959.

Appendix I: Preparation and Submission of Manuscripts

The appearance of a manuscript submitted for consideration is as important as the appearance of a person applying for a job. The right appearance will not sell his story, but at least it will not interfere with its being sold.

The writer should type his manuscript on white bond paper, double spaced, leaving an inch margin on the sides and bottom. He should number his pages either at the top or bottom, and after page one he should type the title of his story on the top left side of each page in capital letters. The author should, of course, make one or more carbon copies.

A short story or an article does not require a separate title page. The writer's legal name and address should be placed at the top left side of the first page. The title of the story, in capital letters, is centered about two inches below the top margin. If the writer wishes, he may write the approximate number of words at the top right side. He does not mention rates, and he does not have to mention rights since these are standard.

Editors prefer to receive unclipped and unstapled manuscripts in manila envelopes. They also want stamped, self-addressed manila envelopes enclosed for the return of the manuscript. Booklength manuscripts should be sent loose in a cardboard box, not in fancy, complicated folders.

Do not:

Send a manuscript written in longhand or single spaced

Send a manuscript typed in any color except black

Enclose a letter telling the editor how excellent your story is, how excellent his magazine is, or how desperately you want to sell your story

A cover letter is useful only if the writer knows the editor or has been in correspondence with him. If the writer has been published previously by this magazine or by other national magazines, he should write a brief note mentioning his other publications.

Letters of inquiry are not necessary for the submission of short stories. However, time and postage can be saved by such letters if the manuscripts are articles, novels, or booklength nonfiction. The letters will include a brief description of the work and the writer's background. To interested magazine editors, the article writer should send the introduction and a detailed outline of his work; the book writer should send two or three chapters and a detailed outline of the rest of the work to publishers who have stated that they are interested in his subject.

It is not ethical to send a completed work to more than one publisher at a time. It is ethical to submit television and film scripts to more than one producer.

Most of the avoidable rejections go to:

1. The writer who submits sloppy, unreadable manuscripts
2. The writer who sends a story to a magazine that does not publish fiction
3. The writer who sends to *Playboy* a story that might interest the editors of *Good Housekeeping,* or vice versa
4. The writer who sends a story to a magazine that has gone out of business

The writer may submit his work directly to a publisher, or he may send it to an agent.

He must forget the words of his friends and relatives who tell him that no one can get published who isn't a "name" writer or who isn't related to the editor or publisher. It is, of course, easier to get published if the writer has already established himself.

However, editors and publishers are constantly looking for new good talent; they are constantly hoping that such talent will come in the morning mail. Editors do read manuscripts from free-lance writers unless they have announced a contrary policy. In this latter case, manuscripts are returned unopened and marked with this announcement.

When the morning mail arrives at a publisher's office, the mail clerk, an office boy, or a secretary sorts the manuscripts. In one pile he puts the obviously unpublishable: handwritten, those written by crackpots, and those with impossibly bad grammar, spelling, and punctuation. These are immediately returned with rejection slips to the writers. In another pile are manuscripts from well-known writers, writers who have been previously published by the magazine, and writers who are in correspondence with the editors. These manuscripts are sent directly to specific editors on the staff. Stories and articles from unknown writers compose the third pile. These are sent to "first readers," who recommend their rejection or suggest that they be read by the editors for possible publication. If rejected, these manuscripts are usually returned with the printed rejection form. If they show some promise, an editor may write a brief note. Rarely does he offer a specific reason for rejection or make editorial suggestions. He cannot afford to get into a lengthy discussion with the writer. If he does recommend certain revisions, it is because he is definitely interested in the manuscript.

This process is often a slow one, particularly if the publication's staff is small. The short-story writer should not become impatient if the magazine holds his story for six weeks or two months. After that length of time, however, he is justified in sending an inquiry. The small literary magazines often hold a story for as long as six months, not out of carelessness but because of the small staff.

About eighty percent of the stories published in magazines are submitted by literary agents. There are several reasons for this. The agent is there; he knows the kind of story the publisher is looking for; and he saves the publisher's staff time and salary. Book and magazine publishing is not richly rewarding like, for example, sugar-packaging and oil-producing. And, it must be admitted, it is sometimes easier to do business with an agent than with a writer.

The agent is equally important to the writer. He is the writer's business representative and is responsible for all business connected with the writer's total literary work. He collects ten percent commission on all sales in return for which he handles the author's work in all fields, including publishing, motion pictures, television, foreign reprints. If he works with a Hollywood agent for motion-picture or television sales, the commission is still only ten percent. The agent does not advertise, nor does he charge a fee for reading material. He does not accomplish miracles; in most cases, he does not instruct, rewrite, or edit. And he is, of course, fallible. He has misses and hits.

Although agents, like publishers, are in constant search of promising writers, they are not always willing to handle the work of an unknown writer. Since theirs is strictly a commercial enterprise, they prefer to represent writers who have some background of publication. Some of them however, are willing to look at freelance writing and take a chance on its success.

A list of literary agents can be obtained from the Authors Guild, 234 W. 44th Street, New York, N.Y. 10016. The majority of literary agents have their offices in New York, but there are a few in the Los Angeles area. Some of the large firms have offices both in New York and in Hollywood. Literary agents are listed in the yellow pages of the telephone directories, but again the unknown writer has trouble finding one who will represent him.

Generally speaking, the agent is interested in fiction rather than nonfiction, in adult fiction rather than juvenile fiction. Most nonfiction writers work directly with the publishers. For this reason it is important for the nonfiction writer to become well acquainted with the publishing companies' specialties.

One final word may be useful to the beginning writer: He must learn how to live with his rejection slips. He must not feel that each is a dagger in his back. On the other hand, he should not look upon them as evidence that great work is never rewarded. He should find out why he gets rejection slips. Once he knows what is wrong, he can set about correcting the wrong. He is then on the road to becoming a published writer.

Appendix II: A Literary Vocabulary

Abstract poetry: Poetry in which the writer selects words, not for their usual meanings, but for the effect produced by their sounds, rhythms, and rhymes. The English poet Edith Sitwell first used the term.

Abstraction: Ideas formed by an intellectual process in which the mind selects characteristics common to a group and reaches a concept that describes all the members of the group. "liberty" is an abstraction. The actual Declaration of Independence and the Liberty Bell are concrete terms. Romeo and Juliet are concrete expressions of the abstraction called "young love." Because abstractions are ideas, they tend to be the language of philosophy and science; the language of literature tends to be more specific, more concrete.

Aesthetic distance: The distance between a writer and the emotional and personal experience that was responsible for his work. Another word for it is objectivity.

Antagonist: The chief enemy of the protagonist or hero. The antagonist may be a human being, an animal, a force of nature, or even a state of mind. He may live inside the protagonist. The antagonist of Hemingway's *The Old Man and the Sea,* for example, is the sea itself. The strength of the antagonist must be as great as or greater than that of the protagonist; otherwise, the writer cannot engage the reader in the conflict.

Anti-hero: The protagonist of much of the literature produced in the 1960s, sometimes called the nonhero. The traditional hero has been a bigger-than-life man, bigger in his virtues and vices than the average man. The anti-hero is likely to be less than life-size in his emotions, ambitions, achievements, dreams, as well as in his physical stature. The protagonist of John Updike's *Rabbit Run* is an example of the anti-hero or nonhero. So is Tommy of Malamud's "The Prison."

Archetype: A character, story, image, or description that has occurred so widely in myth, religion, folklore that it evokes a primordial image in the reader's unconscious memory and a strong, inexplicable response. The term comes from the psychiatrist Jung's belief that the collective unconscious of the human race lies behind every man's unconscious. The repeated experiences of man's ancestors make possible these primordial images in myths, dreams, fantasies. Oedipus, for example, is a character that evokes such primordial images. *Paradise Lost* portrays an archetypal situation.

Atmosphere: The tone of a literary work. It can be established by the physical setting or by the emotional state of mind in the character who opens the story. The tone is sustained throughout the work.

Catharsis: A word used to express the effect of a tragic story upon the reader or spectator. Jung called the tragic hero a symbol, a human figure upon whom we load our emotions and thus free ourselves from our own feelings of grief, anger, and sin. This identification with the tragic hero is catharsis.

Classic: An enduring piece of literature recognized as excellent. *Moby Dick* is an American classic.

Classics: The literary productions of Greece and Rome.

Classicism: A term derived from the Greek and Latin rules for literary standards. These standards included adherence to the three unities (time, place, and action); clarity and simplicity; decorum; reason and restraint; objectivity. The classical point of view was revived by seventeenth-century French writers, Corneille, Racine, Boileau, who in turn influenced English writers of the Restoration and Augustan ages.

Climax: The turning point in the short story, the novel, and the play: the place at which the rising action starts to fall. Usually, but not always, it is the high point of interest. Often it is when the protagonist makes an important decision, a decision that changes his life or keeps it from changing at a future time.

Coherence: A fundamental principle demanding that parts of a piece of writing bear such a relationship to one another that the whole is intelligible, although not necessarily conventional.

Comic relief: A piece of humor used in serious fiction to provide relief from unbearable intensity. This is a nonclassical device. The gravediggers' scene in *Hamlet* is an example.

Connotation: The implication a word or phrase carries with it apart from its precise, dictionary meaning. The writer depends upon connotations for his more profound meanings.

Controlling image: The figure of speech that runs throughout a piece of work.

Convention: A literary device that has become an accepted technique. Shakespeare's monologues and Eugene O'Neill's "asides" are conventions.

Crisis: A step leading up to the climax of a story. Crises are situations involving the protagonist which further complicate the plot.

Cubist poetry: Poetry in which the poet fragments an experience, then rearranges the pieces to give the experience a new meaning. Kenneth Rexroth is, in part, a cubist poet.

Deus ex machina: The use of an unexpected and unbelievable incident to make the story come out right. The classicists used a god for this; today, a bad writer may turn up a long-lost brother to solve a problem, or he may turn the whole story into a dream.

Existentialism: A philosophical school that has been given literary expression by contemporary French writers (Jean Paul Sartre, Simone de Beauvoir, Albert Camus, and others). Existentialism had its beginnings in the writings of the Danish philosopher Kierkegaard, which were later expounded by the German philosopher Heidegger. The basic conviction of the existentialist is that existence precedes essence: that man *is* and then *becomes*, making himself up as he goes along, and is responsible for himself. He is aware of his own situation in an often meaningless and absurd world. Examples of existential literature are Sartre's play *No Exit* and Camus' novel *The Stranger*.

Exposition: A type of composition of particular value to the non-fiction writer. Exposition explains the nature of a person, thing, or idea, mainly by definition, classification, analysis, comparison and contrast, illustration or examples.

Expressionism: An artistic and literary movement that began in Germany early in the twentieth century. It was basically a revolt against realism in the arts and took the form of distortion in time, space, and logic to show how the world really appears to troubled people. Emphasis was taken from individuals and placed on types; stage settings became nonrealistic; and dialogue sounded like telegraphic messages. Eugene O'Neill's *The Emperor Jones* and Elmer Rice's *The Adding Machine* are examples of American expressionism. This anti-realism is also visible in the plays of Thornton Wilder, Tennessee Williams, and Arthur Miller.

Fable: A short tale that points a moral. The characters are usually animals that reflect human characteristics in a satirical manner. The fable has been popular since the time of Aesop in 600 B.C. The best-known modern fable is George Orwell's *Animal Farm*, a satire on totalitarianism.

Fantasy: A work that takes place in an unreal world, suspends known physical laws, and deals with characters who belong to an imagined world. Aldous Huxley's *Brave New World* and George Orwell's *1984* are fantasies. Fantasy is a general term that includes science fiction.

Farce: A kind of comedy depending for its humor on exaggerated situations, low wit, and physical incongruities rather than on character and story. Many of the plays of the Theater of the Absurd are labeled tragi-farces. Pie throwing is an example of the farcical device.

Figurative language: Language that makes an effect through the senses or by comparisons. It creates images by the use of similes, metaphors, personification, and other figures of speech.

Flashback: The dramatic exposition of scenes, situations, or incidents that take place before the opening scene of a short story, novel, or play. It is accomplished through recollections of a character presented dramatically as in Arthur Miller's *After the Fall* or through dream sequences as in Elmer Rice's *Dream Girl.*

Frame story: A story within a story. *The Canterbury Tales*, for example, is a story about a group of people making a pilgrimage. This is the frame. The stories told by the various characters are frame stories. Somerset Maugham frequently used this device by having one person narrate a complete story to another person or a group of people.

Genre: A term used to designate groupings of literary works (novels, plays, short stories, teleplays, poetry, essays) as well as their divisions according to type—comedy, romantic novel, and so on. It is not to be confused with its meaning in painting, which is the realistic presentation of an ordinary or commonplace scene.

Gothic literature: A term applied to a novel which creates an atmosphere of brooding or terror. True gothic was originated in the eighteenth century by Horace Walpole, who used the medieval settings, magic, mystery, and chivalry to establish his atmosphere. *Frankenstein* by Mary Wollstonecraft Shelley is an example of this literary movement that became a part of nineteenth-century romanticism. The word itself is derived from the Germanic tribe of Goths. It later connoted Germanic, then medieval, and finally, for the romanticists, whatever was wild, primitive, free, natural, the antithesis of neoclassicism. In the United States, Edgar Allen Poe is an early representative of the gothic.

Humanism: In general, a point of view that stresses the importance of the human being rather than the gods or gross animal elements. In literature the term was used to designate the revival of classical culture which was part of the renaissance beginning in the fourteenth century. The New Humanism was a critical movement occurring in the United States early in the twentieth century as a reaction against realism and naturalism and as a protest against the philosophies of the scientific age; it was led by Irving Babbitt and Paul Elmer More.

Imagery: Literally, the collection within a piece of writing of images that are concrete representations of sensory experiences. More generally imagery is synonymous with figures of speech, including similes and metaphors. Images may be used so that their meaning is the same for all readers, or they may have different meanings for different people. They may be literal; that is, they may state directly the sensory representation of the object. Or they may be figurative, as are the simile and the metaphor. The appeal of the image is to the sensuous memory of the reader. Patterns of imagery may be keys to the more profound meaning of a literary work.

Impressionism: A term borrowed by writers of the late nineteenth and early twentieth centuries from such French painters as Manet, Monet, and Renoir who, in rebellion against the conventional style of painting, believed it was more important to show the impressions made upon the artist than to give the specific details of the object painted. Instead of painting trees, they painted the effect of a tree. Impressionism in poetry was an important element in the work of the early twentieth-century imagist poets. The English novelist Virginia Woolf is the best example of the fiction impressionist.

Interior monologue: A technique employed to present the stream of consciousness of a character. It is the internal experience of the character on any level of consciousness and may go all the way back to the nonverbal level where images must represent the experience or the emotion. Virginia Woolf effectively used the kind of interior monologue in which the author selects and presents the experiences of the character. James Joyce, in addition to this kind, also made use of the kind of monologue that is given directly by the character to the reader, as if the reader were eavesdropping on a dream or nightmare.

Irony: A figure of speech whose words convey the opposite of the meaning intended by the speaker. An example of sustained irony is Jonathan Swift's "A Modest Proposal" for saving a starving Ireland by suggesting that the Irish sell their children for food to the English landlords. Other examples of irony are Mark Antony's repetition that "Brutus is an honorable man," and Othello's reference to "honest Iago."

Legend: A story handed down from the past. The legend differs from the myth in having more specific historical truth and less of the supernatural. It is likely to express a particular racial or regional spirit.

Local-color writing: The kind of writing which has as its primary purpose to present the people and the life of a certain geographical setting. Local-color writers include Mark Twain, Bret Harte, Lafcadio Hearn, Joel Chandler Harris, and Sarah Orne Jewett. Whimsy and eccentricity often characterize this kind of writing.

Melodrama: A term, originally meaning "a play with music," now referring to a play whose appeal is to the emotions of the audience by any means the writer chooses to use. "Soap opera" on television is the most current and widespread example of melodrama.

Montage: A term borrowed from motion pictures by impressionistic writers to establish atmosphere of a scene by a series of impressions or pictures with no apparent order. Dos Passos used the montage in his "newsreels" for his trilogy *U.S.A.*

Myth: A story whose roots are in primitive folklore and are the product of a racial group rather than an individual storyteller. All countries and literatures have myths which have grown up around certain themes in common: life and death, religion, natural phenomena, and great heroes. With the acceptance by some writers of Jung's concept of the racial unconscious, the myth has been extensively examined in literature by critics who see it as the repository of racial memories and an expression of the general views of a race.

Naturalism: The name of a literary movement of the late nineteenth and early twentieth centuries which called for an application of the principles of scientific determinism to fiction. The assumption is that everything that is real is in nature. For the naturalist writer and philosopher, man is an animal in the natural world who is controlled by environmental forces as well as by internal forces, and the job of the writer is to reveal in the novel his scientific theory of the nature of experience. The real is not important in itself but in what it reveals about a total reality. The naturalist writer therefore selects actual events and experiences and subjects them to a laboratory method of experiment. More loosely, the term "naturalism" is applied to any extreme form of realism and is said to portray man not as he is but as much worse than he is. For the romantics, naturalism was merely a profound interest in nature.

The movement began in France and was given its definition and code by Émile Zola. In the United States it was first represented by Frank Norris and Jack London. The outstanding American naturalist novelist, however, was Theodore Dreiser, author of *An American Tragedy*. This literary school continues to be popular in the United States.

Neoclassicism: The kind of classicism that dominated English literature in the seventeenth and eighteenth centuries, modeled upon Greek and Roman classicism as well as upon the French neoclassical school. Its ideals of classicism were order, restraint, unity, harmony, and good taste. The appeal was to the intellect rather than to the emotions, and didactic literature flourished. The heroic couplet became the major verse form. Major English writers in the neoclassical tradition were Milton, Bunyan, Dryden, Pope, and Johnson. In the twentieth century there has been a neoclassical tendency with its respect for intellect in art. T. S. Eliot is an excellent example of a contemporary neoclassicist.

The New Criticism: A protest against romanticism, expressionism, and impressionism, the New Criticism is a set of doctrines or literary attitudes shared by some twentieth-century critics who consider literature as a valid form of knowledge in itself. The protest has taken the form of the objective theory of art: art for its own sake.

Pathetic fallacy: Originally, a phrase describing writing that invests nature with the emotions of human beings, it also indicates any false emotionalism in writing about nature.

Platonism: The doctrines of the Greek philosopher Plato, which he himself did not formulate into a theory but which have been more or less codified by his followers. Plato's concern with the invisible world of transcendent ideas and with man's destiny and potentialities strongly influenced the Italian renaissance writers and the English romantic poets.

Poetic justice: Formerly, a term meaning that virture was rewarded and vice punished. The more modern meaning among writers is that the resolution and conclusion of a work of literature are inevitable outcomes of the motivations presented by the writer throughout his work, even though vice is not punished and virtue goes unrewarded.

Realism: A literary revolt against romanticism which dominated literature during the first half of the nineteenth century. The realist looks for a truth that can be verified and gives his attention to what is immediate and discernible. His subject materials are the common everyday experiences of average or middle-class people. For the realist, characterization is the most important element in fiction, and plot is secondary. Henry James is the outstanding exponent of realism in America, and the tradition has continued with Edith Wharton, Sinclair Lewis, John O'Hara, John Marquand, and many others.

Romanticism: A school of literature that began in France as a protest against the order, restraint, and didacticism of neo-classicism. Although the movement varied in various countries, it followed certain general changes in expression: love of nature, individualism, a concern with the past, an admiration of the wild and savage, profound interest in human rights, and an abandonment of structural rules.

Romanticism in America produced this country's first highly creative period in literature. The major literary figures concerned with the romantic school were Hawthorne, Melville, Irving, Cooper, Thoreau, Emerson, Poe, Whittier, Lowell, Longfellow, and Whitman. The romantic tradition continues today with any writer who believes in the individual man and his right to freedom from systems and rules.

Stream of consciousness: A term applied to a certain kind of psychological novel whose subject matter is the endless "flow of consciousness" of one or more of its characters. The device used for this kind of verbal expression is "interior monologue," which records the emotional experience of a character on any one level of consciousness or on combinations of such levels. The true stream-of-consciousness novel concentrates on the prespeech level where the image expresses the response. Writers of this kind of novel believe that it is free psychological association, not logic, that determines people's feelings and thoughts and therefore that it is natural to present feelings and thoughts in the illogical and disjointed manner of interior dialogue. Most writers of this school, however, write psychological novels rather than the pure stream-of-consciousness type and employ interior monologues in part.

Index